Reclaiming the Inner City

Chicago's Near North Revitalization
Confronts Cabrini-Green

Ed Marciniak

National Center for Urban Ethnic Affairs
Washington, D.C.

This report was prepared under a grant from the Ford Foundation.

Printed in the United States of America
All Rights Reserved
Library of Congress Catalog Card #85-60740
ISBN-0-940798-05-0

Cover design by Susan Atlas Kelley. Photograph on page 56 is reproduced with the permission of Jonas Dovydenas. Jacob Burck's cartoon on page 99 is reprinted with permission of the *Chicago-Sun Times,* © News Group Chicago, Inc., 1949.

Contents

Chicago's Near North Side

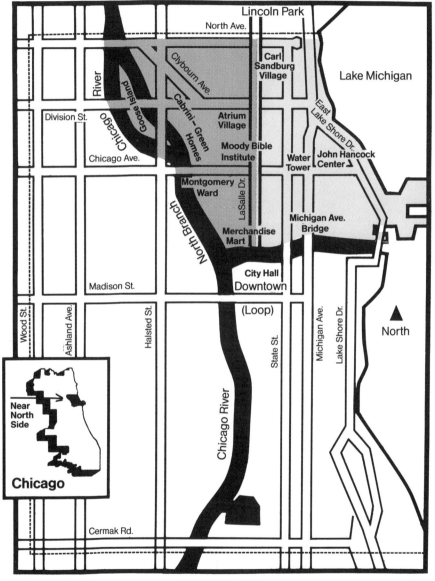

Lower North Side

Gold Coast

------ The boundaries of 'Old Chicago,' that area incorporated as the City of Chicago in 1837, were: North Ave., Wood St., Cermak Rd. and Lake Michigan.

5

Foreword

No doubt we would have had to face up to the issue sooner or later. Because we are doing it later does not ease the task but only makes it more difficult. The *issue* is what to do about the public housing projects in our inner cities and the people that live there.

In Chicago, public housing's 168 family high-rise buildings are monuments to the city's racism and to its ineptitude in facing up to the urgent and ever-present question: how will our society house its poor and powerless? Only a handful of Chicago's civic, educational, business and religious leaders have had the courage or the ability to address the question with more than hand-wringing platitudes.

Yet, at many a social gathering in Chicago or its suburbs, the question will eventually be asked: what do you think can or should be done about Chicago's high-rise public housing? The conversation will elicit biased and wondrous "off the top of one's head" opinions from those who have never come closer to a housing project than speeding by on an adjacent expressway or scanning a newspaper's public housing horror stories.

Such offhand opinions are shredded by Ed Marciniak, a longtime and respected social activist and a professor of urban studies at Chicago's Loyola University. As the quintessential "urban man," Marciniak is a "hands-on" writer, the man who walks and observes the city's streets, while taking an intimate part in what goes on. He understands the special accents and character of each community in a city celebrated for its rich neighborhood life, as well as its ethnic and racial mix. No longer will it be possible for anyone to assess the future of public housing in Chicago — or elsewhere — without studying *Reclaiming the Inner City,* his newest book.

Marciniak can speak eloquently of Chicago's beauty, its history and geography, and especially of its people he loves. This affection steered his attention to the Lower North Side which was rebuilt after the Great Chicago Fire and has since gone through a succession of ethnic and racial changes. Today, the area is all but forgotten except by business entrepreneurs and real estate speculators, by dedicated staffs of religious institutions and public agencies, and by private social service organizations which serve the poor.

Why do the poor remain on the Lower North Side? Because most have no place else to go. This is especially true of the residents of the Cabrini-Green housing project, known the nation over as one of the most disastrous experiments in public housing in the country. But Cabrini-Green is not only a name and a location to Marciniak; he is concerned about its people who are now being hemmed in by the encroachment of prosperity, in one form or another, from three sides. Marciniak invites Chicagoans to take off their blinders and to see what is happening to Cabrini-Green, both outside and inside. There is little sentimentality in this book, but there is common sense. *Reclaiming the Inner City* is scholarship and social analysis at its best.

Marciniak traces the poignant story of the Lower North Side back through the decades when it housed peoples immigrating from foreign shores. The area's successes and bloodletting are vividly unfolded. Economic forces now press relentlessly on the public housing island which shelters the poorest and most powerless in Chicago's society, the inhabitants of Cabrini-Green. Its towers, in which 13,500 people sleep each night, stand in painful contrast to the massive wealth and influence of the Gold Coast which lies immediately to the east and skirts Chicago's fabled lakefront.

While lakefront residents prosper, what is happening to the Cabrini-Green project and its people? Marciniak keeps probing for answers, for a compromise, for brave new thoughts before the massive destruction of the high rises begins. He realizes that a compassionate response to the problem must be found. His book lays out the scene, the actors, the plot and the background with skill and incisive accuracy. Marciniak is too wise to tease us with simplistic answers; that is why he offers hopeful options.

Reclaiming the Inner City can rightfully take its proud place along with two earlier studies Marciniak has published on Chicago communities. These studies, *Reviving an Inner City Community* and *Reversing Urban Decline*, added much to our understanding of a changing Chicago. The current book is a further distillation of his years of study about the future of Chicago and its neighborhoods.

One may or may not have a studied opinion — even an opinion — about public housing in our nation, but this book will educate, stimulate and challenge everyone to take a serious look at Chicago's public housing and the city's values.

Msgr. John J. Egan

Chronology

Milestones in the History
of the Lower North Side, 1929 to 1990

1929   A book by Harvey Zorbaugh, *The Gold Coast and the Slum,* is published, documenting the social and economic conditions of Chicago's Lower North Side. (See map.)

1930   Montgomery Ward & Co. occupies its new eight-story administration building on Chicago Avenue at the Chicago River's North Branch, across the street from its retail store and warehouses.

1930   The Merchandise Mart officially opens.

1930   The Marshall Field Garden Apartments become ready for occupancy in one of the early years of the Great Depression.

1934   The Lower North Center, a social service agency, is organized to serve Italian and black youth in a community with "the second highest incidence of juvenile delinquency" in Chicago.

1943   The first 581 families move into the new row houses of Frances Cabrini Homes, the Lower North Side's first public housing project, built on the site of what once was called "Little Italy."

1951   The Chicago Housing Authority issues *Cabrini Extension Area: Portrait of a Slum,* the report which paves the way for building fifteen high-rise buildings as "a further inroad into one of the oldest slums in the city."

1958   The Chicago Housing Authority erects Cabrini Extension, fifteen high-rise buildings containing 1,896 apartments.

1962   The CHA builds Green Homes, eight high rises holding

1,096 apartments, and the public housing project acquires a new name: Cabrini-Green Homes.

1963   Montgomery Ward & Co. closes its retail store on Chicago Avenue, signaling the decline of the adjoining commercial and industrial area.

1963   Ground is broken for Carl Sandburg Village, a large private housing development on the east side of LaSalle Drive, on land bought and cleared by the Chicago Department of Urban Renewal.

1965   St. Philip Benizi Church, once the religious hub of Little Italy, is demolished.

1968   The Chicago Department of Urban Renewal approves Project Chicago-Orleans, designating the area just east of Cabrini-Green as "a slum and blighted area."

1968   Montgomery Ward & Co. decides to stay on the Lower North Side and builds a new corporate headquarters, twenty-six stories high, on Chicago Avenue across the street from Cabrini-Green.

1968   State Representative Robert L. Thompson, a black, is elected for a first term to the Illinois General Assembly, representing the Lower North Side and adjoining areas. His constituents are predominantly white.

1968   The Moody Bible Institute turns down a proposal to move its campus, including 1,300 full-time students, 2,500 part-timers and a staff of 675, to a Chicago suburb. In 1986 the Institute would celebrate its 100th anniversary at the same location on Chicago Avenue and LaSalle Drive.

1970   A modern church building is dedicated by the St. Matthew United Methodist Congregation to replace a structure badly damaged by fire. The new church is less than a block from Cabrini-Green.

1973   St. Joseph School, located across the street from Cabrini-Green and the last of the four Catholic elementary schools which once served children from Little Italy, marks its 100th anniversary.

1977   Bulldozers prepare the land for the construction of Atrium Village, a private residential development resulting from Project Chicago-Orleans.

1978   The Evergreen-Sedgwick Apartments, the first private housing development for moderate-income families since 1930, begins renting eighty-four low-rise apartments. The sponsor is the Near North Development Corporation, a not-for-profit, self-help group initiated by local black residents. By 1985 the development would contain 268 apartments and encompass ten acres.

1979   The new Near North Career Magnet High School opens, while the old building which housed Cooley Vocational High School is demolished.

1981   Both the YMCA and St. Joseph Hospital open new facilities on the south side of North Avenue.

1981   Cabrini-Green gains world-wide notoriety during the brief sojourn of Mayor Jane Byrne and her husband, Jay McMullen, as apartment residents.

1982   LaSalle Street Church celebrates the 100th anniversary of its building. The church's history, according to 42nd Ward Alderman Burton Natarus, "is a veritable mirror of the changes which have occurred" on the Lower North Side.

1982   The *Chicago Tribune* transfers its printing and circulation operations and 1,800 full-time workers to a new facility on the west bank of the Chicago River's North Branch and across the river from Montgomery Ward & Co.

1983   Oscar Mayer Foods Corporation and its 1,100 employees mark the 100th year of the company's presence on the Lower North Side.

1990   The CHA has vacated its first Cabrini-Green high rise. The building is either recycled for some other use or destroyed.

1

Defying the
Urban Pessimists

*Chicago is the glory and damnation
of America all rolled up into one.
Not to know Chicago is not to know
America.* —Neal R. Peirce and Jerry
Hagstrom, *The Book of America*

Civic pessimists belong to an ancient profession. For millenia they have deplored cities and rejoiced in their disintegration. As the oldest urban minority, such cynics voiced misgivings as early as the Book of Genesis, whose author recounts how the patriarch Abraham combed the streets of Sodom and Gomorrah in search of ten honest citizens. When Abraham defaulted on his divine contract to produce the ten, Sodom and Gomorrah found themselves with a worthless past and no future. The cities self-destructed.

On the eastern seaboard of the United States, in the middle of the 19th century, Boston's VIPs feared inundation from a flood of new immigrants. New England's Anglo-Saxon establishment watched in horror as boatloads of women and men from famine-wracked Ireland choked Boston's harbor. The disembarking passengers soon clogged Boston's streets and shantytowns, bawling in unfamiliar speech rhythms and offering obeisance to an unwelcome religion. Hoping to rescue the city from the Irish invasion, Boston Brahmins huddled frantically on Beacon Hill, where they wailed: "Boston has no future; the Irish will engulf us." But the proper Bostonians failed to halt the Irish intruders. Many of the upper crust fled to new

housing in neighboring Cambridge. In 1885 Hugh O'Brien, the first
of a long line of Irish mayors, took office. Despite the earlier fears
of its urban elite, Boston not only survived the immigrant flood of
the 19th century but now thrives in the 20th.

Urban pessimists celebrated a victory of sorts in 1871, this time on
the sandy beaches of Lake Michigan near the mouth of the Chicago
River. On October 19th of that year, the *Chicago Evening Journal*
reported:

> Chicago is burning! Up to this hour of writing (1 o'clock p.m.) the
> best part of the city is already in ashes! An area between six and
> seven miles in length and nearly a mile in width, embracing the
> great business part of the city, has been burned over and now lies a
> mass of smouldering ruins!
>
> All the principal hotels, all the public buildings, all the banks, all
> the newspaper offices, all the places of amusement, nearly all the
> great business edifices, nearly all the railroad depots, the water
> works, the gas works, several churches, and thousands of private
> residences and stores have been consumed. The proud, noble,
> magnificent Chicago of yesterday is today a mere shadow of what
> it was; and, helpless before the still sweeping flames, the fear is
> the entire city will be consumed before we see the end.

Editorial comment from other cities was not always sympathetic.
As the fire burned through 21,124 acres, seventy-three miles of
streets and 18,000 buildings, leaving one-third of Chicago's 334,000
residents homeless, a New Orleans newspaper predicted:

> Chicago will never be like Carthage of old. Its glory will be of the
> past, not the present, while its hopes once so bright and cloudless
> will be to the end marred and blackened by the smoke of its fiery
> fate.

Recalling Chicago's reputation as a town wide open to bawdy-
houses and gambling, a St. Louis newspaper editor passed this judg-
ment on Chicago's future: "Again the fire of heaven has fallen on
Sodom and Gomorrah!"

The Missouri editor, however, was denied his vengeance. Out of
the mud banks and charred ruins a new city developed at the lake.
Before long, the city readied itself for a dazzling World's Colum-
bian Exposition to be held in 1893. By then, two decades after the
fire, Chicago's population had tripled to more than a million, three
times that of St. Louis. Today St. Louis, which had been the

nation's third most populated city in 1870 and Chicago's chief rival as the gateway to the West, is 27th in size.

The doomsday talk continues. In 1974 an urban geographer, then stationed at the Chicago campus of the University of Illinois, lamented: "America's cities are sick, if not dying." In his urban obituary, he listed Chicago. About the same time, a visiting anthropologist from Princeton University in New Jersey told the students at the very same campus: "I see no hope for big cities; there is no reason they should continue to exist. They are disaster areas where human beings cannot be fulfilled."

The Lower North Side

In Chicago, the community singled out by the latest generation of urban pessimists is the Lower North Side. Those three words, Lower North Side, specify an area just north of the Chicago River, which embraces nearly two square miles of the city's inner core. The Lower North Side stakes its claim to a history as old as Chicago's, having been part of that original

> piece of land six miles square at the mouth of the Chicago River emptying into the Southwest end of Lake Michigan. [As ceded by Indians, mostly of the Potawatomi tribe, in the Treaty of Grenville in 1795.]

The area now called the Lower North Side was also part of the original ten square miles and 4,170 residents incorporated as the City of Chicago in 1837. (See map.)

The Lower North Side is not just a parcel of land unceremoniously planted among modern Chicago's 228 square miles. During the Great Fire of 1871, practically every block of this historic urban real estate was left in ashes and ruins. Nothing remained that would remind a later generation that early Chicago was centered, in part, on the Lower North Side. No landmarks. No bridges. No historic buildings. Not even a monument.

Once part of the original Chicago, the Lower North Side today adjoins the "downtown" area which is the center of commerce and government. Its southern boundary is the Chicago River. The western border is again the river which forks at Wolf Point, one branch flowing northward. In the North Branch's path is Goose Island, a land area of sixteen square blocks, a warren of former tanneries, factories and abandoned rail yards, the only island within the city limits. (The island obtained its name in the 19th century from the "watch geese" that guarded the island's gardens and small farms before they were displaced by industry.) The northern limit, the city's original northern edge, is called, prosaically enough, North Avenue. The Lower North Side's eastern edge is LaSalle Drive, which separates the area from Chicago's Gold Coast, a wealthy neighborhood situated next to Lake Michigan. As irresistibly as any Mediterranean resort, the beauty of Chicago's shoreline attracts the rich and mighty. (See map.)

The urban cynics will not let anyone forget that the Lower North Side coincides with the Chicago "slum" spotlighted in 1929 by Harvey Warren Zorbaugh in his classic study contrasting the adjoining areas: *The Gold Coast and the Slum.* He described the Lower North Side "as a slum, without fear of contradiction."

The Lower North Side's past is inseparable from the history of early Chicago. But what about the future? During the second half of the 20th century, Chicago struggles to rebuild its churning center, that historic area incorporated as a city in 1837. The Lower North Side is not only part of that "old Chicago" but is currently burdened by the "slum" heritage chronicled in detail by Zorbaugh. In the last decades of this century, the Lower North Side suffers the throes of uncertain rejuvenation.

A community socially and economically disturbed, the Lower North Side presents older urban America in miniature. There is, of course, evidence of old age and decay: acres of vacant lots covered with broken glass and rubbish, stacks of high-rise public housing and skid row taverns and welfare offices. But to focus on this urban clutter and on the disappearance of familiar institutions, landmarks and ethnic churches merely highlights residential dilapidation while missing the revitalization. On the Lower North Side, there are clearly rhythms of new life. Old and new confront each other each time a youngster looks through the window of a modern elementary or secondary school at an empty, boarded-up building or vacant warehouse. Rehabilitated buildings shadow storefront churches, and new private housing encroaches upon barren land awaiting development. Dead real estate is being reborn.

If the area known as the Lower North Side can be revitalized and shuck its tattered image, urban pessimists will once again be routed. The Lower North Side, with the Cabrini-Green public housing project at its center, is a microcosm of the future of Chicago.

2

Port of Entry

What are the roots that clutch, what
branches grow out of this stony
rubbish?—T.S. Eliot, *The Waste Land*

Any assessment of the Lower North Side's future is shaped by its past, its history as a "port of entry" for successive waves of newcomers who displaced those that had come earlier. The new arrivals, who came from abroad in the 19th century or from the Deep South in the 20th, settled here and, pressed by a newer in-migration, moved elsewhere. The hallmarks of the Lower North Side have always been these: new cultures brandishing foreign languages, poverty with up-and-out mobility, houses within walking distance of factories, long hours at low wages in labor-intensive industry, as well as residential instability and changing institutions. Some understanding of the importance of the Lower North Side as a port of entry can be gleaned from episodes in its history.

● Even before Chicago was incorporated as a city, English traders and settlers had made a home for themselves here and watched the Potawatomi Indians and the French depart.

● The fast-growing city shed its frontier image as the Irish, Germans and Swedes arrived in the decades just before and after the U.S. Civil War. The Lower North Side residents who then sloshed through its muddy streets were mostly foreign born. English, if they could speak or write it, was their second language. Chicago's civic leaders were not astonished when the Lower North Side eventually became the site of the notorious "Kilgubbin." This densely popu-

17

lated settlement of Irish-born immigrants and squatters was described by *The Chicago Times* in 1865 in such picturesque sentences as:

> The Kilgubbin has. . .been the terror of constables, sheriffs and policemen. . . . It numbered several years ago many thousand inhabitants, of all ages and habits, besides droves of geese, goslings, pigs and rats. It was a safe retreat for criminals, policemen not venturing to invade its precincts, or even cross the border, without having a strong reserve force.

Did the newspaper's extravagant rhetoric also conceal an anti-Irish sentiment? In those decades prejudice against newly arriving Irish Catholics was quite open and hostile.

By 20th century standards, the Lower North Side, prior to the Great Chicago Fire of 1871, would have been depicted as an area of deep and abiding poverty. In the immigrant aspirations of the early 19th century, however, the Lower North Side was a port of entry, a place of unprecedented opportunity, a stop on the road to the American dream. For European immigrants, the Kilgubbin settlement offered a temporary home, a small price to pay for religious, political and cultural freedom.

● After the fire of 1871, the commercial and neighborhood patterns of previous decades on the Lower North Side were repeated. Warehouses, retail shops, tanneries, lumber mills, coal yards and manufacturing plants sprang up alongside wooden homes, whose "outhouses" serving as outside toilets could be seen on the alleys or beneath vaulted sidewalks. Despite the new construction, the Lower North Side soon became, once again, a smoke-ridden tract disfigured by unpaved, muddy streets. It came to be called, affectionately, Smoky Hollow.

● The Irish were eventually supplanted by immigrants from Italy. Four separate Catholic parishes were organized: Assumption, St. Dominic, St. Philip Benizi and San Marcello. A priest whose grandparents had come to Chicago from Sicily shares this insight:

> Each parish served a different group of immigrant families who came here from Tuscany, Genoa or Sicily. Over there they were not Italians. It was only here in the United States that they were incorrectly bunched as Italians.

> The same mistake is being made nowadays with newcomers from Puerto Rico, Mexico, Cuba, Brazil, Peru, Ecuador and elsewhere

on the South American continent. We call them Hispanics, Latinos or Chicanos. They are not Hispanics. It is we who label them, lump them together — even though each of their cultures, history and nationalities is singular.

The Kilgubbin had been replaced by Little Sicily and Little Hell. In the early 1900s, Little Sicily gained notoriety because of frequent news accounts of bombings, stabbings and shootings. Murders, it was said, were rarely solved. Historian Rudolph J. Vecoli noted that because of Little Sicily's sinister reputation, its residents "were often barred from employment and had difficulty moving into other neighborhoods."

But in the years prior to World War I, there was another side to Little Sicily, often overlooked. Today's "old-timers," as Anne Keegan wrote in the *Chicago Tribune*, recall it fondly as

> the "old neighborhood," speaking Italian, keeping the old customs and doing things the hard way. . . .There were no public housing projects then; there were rickety two- and three-story buildings with Italians looking for work and a future. Everyone knew it was St. Philip Benizi parish. The sidewalks were wooden, the streets were wooden, the toilets were outside and underneath the street. No one had indoor plumbing. The kids got in the washtubs on Saturday nights. The adults went to public bathhouses on Saturday morning. . . .They are the ones from the old country who looked for dreams and found hard work. Hard work is what they gave, a close family is what they got in return.

● In the decades immediately following World War I, southern blacks began moving into old and deteriorating buildings on the edge of Little Italy. Soon "slum clearance" ousted many Italian families to make room for new public housing which brought additional blacks into the area. The Lower North Side was left with four Italian churches but few traditional parishioners. As the remaining Swedes and Germans left, a colony of Persians from Asia Minor was established; soon they too departed.

In the late 1920s, the Lower North Side was still a port of entry and had become an area which Zorbaugh could describe

> as a slum, without fear of contradiction. For this area, cut off by the barrier of river and industry and for years without adequate transportation, has long been a backwater in the life of the city. This slum district is drab and mean. . . . families are living in one or two basement rooms. . . . These rooms are stove heated, and

wood is sold on the streets in bundles, and coal in small sacks. The
majority of the houses, back toward the river, are of wood, not a
few have windows broken out. Smoke, the odor from the gas
works, and the smell of dirty alleys is in the air. . . . The slum har-
bors many sorts of people: the criminal, the radical, the bohe-
mian, the migratory worker, the immigrant, the unsuccessful, the
queer and unadjusted. . . . The foreign colony, on the other
hand, is found in the slum, not because the immigrant seeks the
slum, nor because he makes a slum of the area in which he settles,
but merely because he finds there cheap quarters in which to live,
and little opposition to his coming.

The common denominator of the [Lower North Side] slum is its
submerged aspect and its detachment from the city as a whole.
The slum is a bleak area of segregation of the sediment of society;
an area of extreme poverty, tenements, ramshackle buildings, of
evictions and evaded rents; an area of working mothers and children, of high rates of birth, infant mortality, illegitimacy, and
death; an area of pawnshops and second-hand stores, of gangs, of
"flops" where every bed is a vote.

Closing the Port of Entry

During the Great Depression of the 1930s, however, the Lower
North Side's historic function as a reception center for new arrivals
to the city became obsolete. Newcomers to Chicago dwindled in
number. After World War II those that came settled elsewhere in
the city or suburbs.

Elected officials in City Hall and business leaders downtown had,
for more than a century, ignored the Lower North Side. It lay across
the Chicago River, out of sight and out of mind. Their first priority
was the commercial vitality of downtown itself and the building
boom under way north of the river but near the lakefront. As the
downtown business district prospered and expanded, its leadership
could no longer afford to neglect the Lower North Side, that sagging
residential and commercial area so close to the city's business and
governmental center.

To reclaim the Lower North Side, the first steps were taken in the
early 1930s to link its destiny to that of downtown. Those steps
downplayed the Lower North Side's historic role as a port of entry
for the city's new arrivals.

3

Renewal or Ruin?

Things are never what they seem
Skim milk masquerades as cream.
—Sir William Gilbert

Confounding the urban pessimists, Chicago took giant steps to rejuvenate the Lower North Side during the Great Depression. When the stock market crashed in the fall of 1929, Chicago held onto its traditional optimism. Confidence rippled through the city. To celebrate the 100th anniversary of its incorporation as a village, Chicago hosted another world's fair in 1933 and 1934. Called "A Century of Progress," it attracted 39 million visitors and, despite a world-wide economic depression, was an amazing financial success. As the railroad center of the North American continent, Chicago was able to provide inexpensive and easy access to visitors in an era when the airplane and auto were not yet dominant. On their way to the fair, millions of visitors streamed through the six great train stations which rimmed Chicago's downtown area.

It was logical, then, that Chicago's business leaders would try to reclaim the urban jungle which had overrun the Lower North Side and which was only a few blocks from their corporate offices. Four large, brick-and-mortar projects were inaugurated — two commercial and two residential — even though unemployment was high, prices and wages were falling, and business had slackened.

1. Merchandise Mart

The first project, the Merchandise Mart, established in 1930 a crucial beachhead at the southern edge of the Lower North Side.

21

The world's largest commercial building at that time, the Mart was built by Marshall Field and Company on the north bank of the Chicago River and faced south — toward the central business district located just across the river. The Mart wanted to identify with the economically sound downtown. A real estate developer noted that in the 1930s:

> The Mart hid the Lower North Side from the northern view of City Hall and the downtown bankers. As they looked north, all they could see was the Merchandise Mart. The land behind the Mart, by and large, had been written off by them as "dead real estate," with little future for profitable development, commercial or residential.

The Mart was an eighteen-story colossus which covered two city blocks and was topped by a tower that rose another seven stories. Built on the air rights above the Chicago and Northwestern Railroad tracks, the Mart contained ninety acres of floor space, seven miles of corridors and jobs for over 20,000 people. The "store for storekeepers" could handle over one hundred freight cars beneath the Mart away from street traffic. It had its own bank and post office, as well as drug stores, restaurants to feed 10,000 people and a rapid transit station. An out-of-town reporter characterized the Mart's size aptly and succinctly: "There are mountains smaller than that in Virginia." But the most important effect of the Mart's location was that it extended the edge of the central business district *north* of the Chicago River, reaching into the Lower North Side.

2. Montgomery Ward

The second commercial development was also completed in 1930, less than a mile north of the Merchandise Mart, on the east bank of the North Branch of the Chicago River. Headquartered at this location since 1909, Montgomery Ward & Co., the giant mail order house, was easily the largest single employer on the Lower North Side. Here was Ward's home office, together with a large retail store and a succession of warehouses for its booming catalog business. Ward's executives erected their new corporate headquarters at the North Branch of the Chicago River on Chicago Avenue, the area's principal east-west commercial street. Atop the new building's white, stuccoed art deco tower, they placed a bronze statue, their symbol for Chicago and Montgomery Ward. Margot Gayle wrote in *Chicago History* magazine:

> . . .the bronze statue on top of the. . .Montgomery Ward head-
> quarters building on West Chicago Avenue. . .is Ward's time-
> honored symbol, The Spirit of Progress, a female figure poised
> on her left foot, holding a torch in her right hand and a caduceus,
> an ancient symbol of commerce, in the other, while She leans
> forward in the wind as though to take flight.

If the Lower North Side today displays any landmark, other than the Merchandise Mart, it is this bronze, sixteen-foot statue which dominates the skyline along the North Branch.

3. Marshall Field Garden Apartments

The first large-scale effort to upgrade housing on the Lower North Side was another private initiative, the Marshall Field Garden Apartments which were completed by 1930. They were located in the Lower North Side's north central section, an area stereotyped then as the "run-down Italian neighborhood." Rows of wooden houses and shacks were demolished to make room for ten new buildings with 628 apartments. A Chicago architect recalled fifty years later:

> This was Chicago's first large "urban renewal project." But it
> was privately sponsored, from the very beginning. Without the
> power of eminent domain, the private developer had to acquire
> sixty-five separate parcels of land at a total cost three times the
> original estimate. That hurt. The high land costs made it harder to
> avoid an operating deficit. The brick and concrete buildings were
> well designed. Today they look good and sturdy — and structur-
> ally sound.

The Marshall Field Garden Apartments covered two city blocks and accommodated ten handsome buildings. Each building had laundry and storage rooms; eight had roof gardens and sun rooms. Some buildings also housed large meeting and recreation rooms. To keep rents reasonable and reduce maintenance cost, the five-story buildings were erected without elevators.

The housing development was a philanthropic venture of the estate of Marshall Field, the tycoon who founded the department store empire which bears his name. His grandson, Marshall Field III, who spent his grandfather's money liberally and for liberal causes, spearheaded the slum clearance. His goal was to catalyze the renovation of the surrounding neighborhood by tearing down substandard houses and replacing them with new moderate-income housing. In the genteel language of *Architectural Record* magazine:

> The purpose of the Marshall Field Garden Apartments. . .was to provide moderate-price living quarters to a selected tenancy close to the downtown section. This involved building in an area where the surroundings were not of the standards desired within the apartments.

However, in the blunt words of the professors who compiled the *Local Community Fact Book:*

> This project did not. . .provide better housing for families in the blighted section, since the rents were too high.

A former occupant of the Marshall Field Garden Apartments did not hesitate to rebut the professors:

> Those academics attributed to Marshall Field a purpose which he never had. The wooden firetraps around my building deserved to be torn down. That would save the lives of many kids. The wood- and coal-burning stoves were dangerous. During the winter, I dreaded the clang of fire engines. They were not coming to my building, I knew, but to frame houses nearby, crowded with tiny children.

> Were the rents high, I would not have lived there, walking up to my fifth floor apartment at least once a day. By any standard my rent was moderate, like my income. As an office secretary employed downtown, I often walked to work, saving a few quarters which were hard to come by. Where else could I find a three-room apartment that was clean, fireproof and within walking distance of the zoo in Lincoln Park and the beaches of Lake Michigan?

4. Cabrini Homes

The first three improvements were private initiatives; the fourth, the row houses of Frances Cabrini Homes, were built and operated by the Chicago Housing Authority, a municipal corporation. The planning for this public housing site had begun during the Great Depression. By 1943, all 581 families had moved in. Initially, rental priority was given to wartime workers and their families. The project was named after Mother Frances Cabrini, a nun and the first American citizen to be canonized in Rome. Earlier in the century, she had given medical care to the Italian immigrants who packed the Lower North Side.

Located in the heart of the Lower North Side, the Cabrini Homes project was built down the street from Montgomery Ward & Company's offices, stores and warehouses. Creeping blight had pushed out the pageantry of Little Sicily and would eventually close down the parish of St. Philip Benizi, which had ministered to Sicilian immigrants for half a century. Because it had earlier been the site of the Kilgubbin and later of Little Hell, businessmen dubbed this crime-ridden neighborhood a "jungle."

Devereux Bowly, Jr., author of *The Poorhouse: Subsidized Housing in Chicago, 1895-1976,* described the old housing that was torn down:

> Before redevelopment, the area was an infamous slum. Of the buildings on the site, . . .50 per cent were of frame construction. Of the 683 units on the site, 443 had no bath tubs, 480 had no hot water, and 515 were heated only by stoves. Forty-three toilets were shared by two families each; there were twenty-nine yard toilets and ten "under sidewalk" toilets.

Many of the homes razed to make room for the new brick housing were originally "temporary" shelters. Most lots had two houses on them, one in front and another in the rear on the alley. Built shortly after the Chicago Fire of 1871 to house its homeless victims, many of the "temporaries" were still around and inhabited seventy years later. Cheap, frame buildings, they were flimsily built, structurally deficient and firetraps. Sixty-eight per cent of the units were dilapidated. Illegal conversions were common; in some cases a floor area of 600 square feet had been cut up into four flats, each with its own stove. This shabby section of the Lower North Side had been described by Harvey Zorbaugh as a

> belt of bleak, barren, soot-begrimed, physically deteriorated neighborhoods. . . . The tenement area is the worst of foreign tongues and cultures; the area of cheap lodging houses is a jungle of human wreckage.

The Chicago Housing Authority made its own survey of the area. Later in a report entitled, *Cabrini Extension Area: Portrait of a Slum,* the CHA noted that this "congested slum [site] had the dubious honor of being one of Chicago's oldest slums."

The new Frances Cabrini Homes consisted of 581 apartments in fifty-five low-rise buildings wedged into two square blocks. Built in rows of two- and three-story buildings, Cabrini Homes resembled army barracks. In the late 1940s, seventy-five per cent of the families in Cabrini Homes were white. But the surrounding area was only twenty per cent white, striking evidence of the racial change which had overtaken the Lower North Side.

When Cabrini Homes was first occupied, most households enjoyed fathers who were employed. Public welfare families and single-parent families were the exception. However, as white families left in the 1950s, their apartments were rented to low-income black households on public assistance.

In the late 1940s the Chicago Housing Authority viewed its mission as rescuing low-income residents from dilapidated housing and protecting local institutions from the threat of further urban decay. With considerable pride and optimism, the CHA regarded the Cabrini project as the first step in the rejuvenation of the Lower North Side. The CHA staff saw themselves as improving the quality of housing for black families and offering Chicagoans another opportunity to reduce racial segregation in the city's housing market. As an agent of urban change, the CHA hailed the Cabrini row houses as a new community "just being born. . .an inroad into one of the oldest slums of the city. . . .[Cabrini Homes] stands like a challenge to the existing decay." Because Cabrini was racially integrated, the *Chicago Defender,* the city's black-owned daily newspaper, welcomed it and announced ecstatically that Little Hell was being converted into a "seventh heaven" for blacks. As if officiating at a wake, the *Chicago Defender* editorialized that Little Hell had died. . ."with its numerous murders, high delinquency rates. . . ." It was a decade of high hopes for public housing.

In the Interim

Most of the residential and commercial improvements calculated to reclaim the Lower North Side appeared during the economic depression of the 1930s. Consequently, their impact was delayed at first by the doldrums generated by that depression and subsequently by the nation's preoccupation with World War II. That war not only sent U.S. soldiers into battle in the Far East, Africa and Europe but also lifted the nation — and Chicago — out of the worst depression in the nation's history. During these two decades the Lower North Side's residential and commercial sections stagnated. This situation, by and large, changed little during the 1950s. It was not until the 1960s, therefore, that the impact of the four large projects, built decades earlier to anchor the Lower North Side, could be assessed. Did any of them, as was planned, spur the area's revitalization?

The Four Developments Revisited

The Merchandise Mart, once the world's largest commercial building, had in the early 1940s become the nation's largest white elephant. Financial troubles arising from the Great Depression resulted in a change of ownership. In 1945 Joseph P. Kennedy of Boston bought the Mart at a bargain price of $13 million. By the 1960s, the Kennedy patriarch had not only helped his son, John, become the first Roman Catholic to be elected to the U.S. presidency, but had also turned the Mart into a spectacular merchandising success. In the late 1960s, the Kennedy family began planning a major expansion of the Mart through an Apparel Center to be built across the street. Though it continued to be downtown's foothold on the Lower North Side, the Mart found that its impact upon the blighted commercial buildings to its north was negligible.

Montgomery Ward & Co. emerged in the 1960s as a giant, multinational corporation in a city that had become the world's mail order capital. Cramped for space in an administration building built for a 1930s retail volume, Ward's top executives anguished in the late 1960s over the location of a new corporate headquarters. It would have to provide more office space as well as enhance the corporate image. A Montgomery Ward official reflected on the choice:

> Should the company, or at least its top executives, desert the crumbling commercial and residential neighborhood in its front-yard and relocate elsewhere? To downtown or to the suburbs? Or should it stay put — close to its twenty-six acre complex of warehouses, parking lots, retail stores, catalog house and other offices, all adjoining the North Branch of the Chicago River?

The proponents of flight — inside Ward's executive suite — could quote from a 1966 internal corporate memorandum that presented Ward's view of the Lower North Side:

> The area west of LaSalle Street, our neighborhood, . . . houses. . .a large number of unemployables, anti-social groups. . . .some of the worst syndicate-controlled dives, dope peddlers and liquor-law violators are part of the fabric of the community. Parts of the area are slums that must be cleared;

parts are "dead" business districts that are subject to demolition
and clearance. . . .

Neither this memorandum nor others like it deterred Robert (Tom)
E. Brooker, Montgomery Ward's chief executive officer. It was he
who made the decision to stay and expand in the early 1960s. Two
decades later he recalled that it was not a difficult choice to make:

> We had an excellent, central location and good transportation.
> We could offer free parking to our several thousand employees.
> And there was the possibility of a new subway with an under-
> ground stop at our front door.
>
> City Hall was reliable, easy to work with and interested in
> helping, not hindering. The political environment was stable.

Ward's ultimate decision to stay — and build a new, modern
headquarters — was to have far-reaching consequences for the
Lower North Side. (The new corporate headquarters, located on
Chicago Avenue across the street from Cabrini-Green, was
completed and occupied in the middle 1970s.)

By the middle 1960s the two residential projects, the Marshall
Field Garden Apartments and Cabrini-Green, were in deep trouble.
The Marshall Field Garden Apartments had changed ownership
along with the name several times, from Town and Garden Apartments to Old Town Gardens and then to Town & Gardens. The
name changes failed to upgrade the housing development's image as
a desirable residential complex. Furthermore, the complex did not
satisfy the financial expectations of developers and investors.
Repeated efforts to attract more middle-income households of all
races, in order to maintain racial diversity, proved unsuccessful.
The renamed apartments had become occupied mainly by low-
income black households, many on public assistance. Richard C.
Wade and Harold M. Mayer concluded, in *Chicago: Growth of a
Metropolis,* that "by mid-1967 this development. . .had badly
deteriorated, and its future was uncertain."

In the middle 1960s it was clear that the Lower North Side had
been saturated with public housing. (See Table I.) Three thousand
additional public housing units, all in elevator buildings, had been
added to the original Frances Cabrini row houses. The new family
apartments were in the Cabrini Extension of fifteen high rises and in
the Green Homes (named after William Green, the president of the

American Federation of Labor in the 1930s and 1940s) with eight high-rise buildings.

In the twenty-five years since 1943, public housing owned and operated by the CHA had transformed the residential character of the Lower North Side. By 1968 the original Cabrini row houses had changed

- from a public housing site covering sixteen acres to seventy acres;
- from fifty-five to eighty buildings, ranging from two- and three-story row houses to nineteen-story buildings;
- from a density of 80,000 persons per square mile to 160,000 (New York City, the nation's most crowded city, only had a population density of 23,000 persons per square mile.);
- from a public housing population of 2,000 to 18,000;
- from a racial mix eighty per cent white to a population almost solidly black;
- from predominantly two-parent families to households mostly headed by a single parent; and
- from a vacancy rate of one per cent to a rate in excess of thirteen per cent.

The Cabrini-Green housing project, which had been designed with fanfare to replace one of Chicago's worst slums, spawned a new slum. Public housing's planners had failed to anticipate the unintended consequences of high-rise living for low-income families.

Table I

LOWER NORTH SIDE PUBLIC HOUSING: 1943 - 1968

Name	Year Built	Housing Units
Cabrini Homes	1943	581
Cabrini Extension	1958	1,896
Green Homes	1962	1,096
Flannery Apts. (seniors)	1965	252
Total Units		3,825*

*These units do not include any of the more than 1,000 federally subsidized apartments in privately owned buildings, which would be on the Lower North Side by 1986. (*Source:* Chicago Housing Authority.)

Depopulating Chicago and the Lower North Side

During the 1960s, while the nation's conscience agonized over the civil rights of black Americans and the U.S. role in Vietnam, Chicago faced agonies of its own. The postwar exodus of Chicago residents to the suburbs was seen as a caravan without an end. The tide of European immigrants had subsided. While the movement of new migrants, blacks from the South and Puerto Ricans from their Caribbean island, was sizable, the rush from Chicago to its suburbs was even greater.

Table II

LOWER NORTH SIDE: POPULATION
1940-1980, COMPARED WITH CHICAGO*

| | Lower North Side | | | Chicago |
Year	Total	Black	White & Other	Total
1940	31,317	4,815	26,502	3,376,483
1950	37,616	16,707	20,909	3,620,962
1960	33,350	21,276	12,074	3,550,404
1970	27,978	24,783	3,195	3,369,359
1980	21,772	19,531	2,241	3,005,061

*Between 1950 (the peak year) and 1980, the Lower North Side's population dropped by forty-two per cent, while Chicago's population as a whole decreased by only seventeen per cent. In 1950 Chicago's population had reached 3,620,962, the largest in its history, and began declining thereafter. In 1950 the Lower North Side contained 1.0 per cent of the city's residents; in 1980, 0.7 per cent. (*Source:* U.S. Bureau of the Census.)

After more than a century of spectacular expansion, Chicago's residential growth peaked before 1960. Urban pessimists were again predicting the city's death. As Mayer and Wade noted in *Chicago: Growth of a Metropolis:*

> The pessimists did not seem entirely wrong during the first postwar decade. While the suburbs flourished, the city languished; while new shopping centers sprouted up all around the municipal boundaries, not a single major building went up.

By 1970, for the first time, the population in the suburbs circling the city of Chicago outnumbered the city's residents. Accelerating this trend were the five expressways: Edens, Eisenhower, Kennedy,

Dan Ryan and Stevenson. Each linked Chicago's center with the suburban hinterland and provided the framework for a new metropolis, called by some "Chicagoland." Chicago O'Hare International Airport, located at the northwest edge of the city, was dedicated by President John F. Kennedy in 1963. It soon became the busiest airport in the world. Residential, hotel and commercial development quickly surrounded it, inside and outside the city limits. As it had a century earlier, Chicago still enjoyed the transportation advantages of a strategic North American location. The second largest city in the United States, Chicago sported the nation's heaviest concentration of air, rail and water transportation.

Between 1950 and 1980 the city's population decreased by seventeen per cent. That of the Lower North Side also slid after 1950 — but more precipitously — by forty-two per cent, a loss of nearly 16,000 people. (See Table II.) The decline would have been far greater had the Lower North Side not been given an additional infusion of 3,200 new public housing units. (See Table I.)

The constant turnover in population unsettled the Lower North Side's neighborhood network — its schools, churches, businesses and political institutions. One school principal lamented:

> Have you ever tried to run an elementary school where thirty-five per cent of the students each year are new? Revolving door education is second-rate. You must believe it.

A Devastated Land

Between 1930 and 1970 hundreds of older buildings were demolished and never replaced. Some were abandoned and then destroyed because they were dangerous. Others were removed to allow commercial and institutional expansion. The City's Department of Urban Renewal razed many, hoping to recruit developers who would build on the cleared land. Other buildings just collapsed from fire or age. The only new residential buildings being constructed were public housing projects. The dense tenements were disappearing slowly but surely, leaving acres and acres of vacant, rubbish-strewn land. Ninety per cent of the Lower North Side's houses which had been there in 1930 had been destroyed by 1970. While sections of the Lower North Side looked like a wasteland, residential development was taking place elsewhere in the city.

The Lower North Side's commercial strips deteriorated even further, except for those at the southern edge along the Chicago

River and close to the Merchandise Mart, and those in "Old Town," a glittery gulch of shops and restaurants located in the northeast corner of the area. At a YMCA meeting in 1965 a local merchant voiced his worries:

> Ghost towns once could be found only in distressed rural areas or in coal mining country. But the business streets of the Lower North Side now resemble a ghost town. The better offices and stores have shut down. Insurance coverage at reasonable rates is a delusion. Credit? It's dried up. Peep shows and sleazy taverns are everywhere. So are the prostitutes and drug pushers. Extortion by youth gangs is a threat to my customers. Store window displays, if there are any, look shabby and dingy. Folding iron gates are in every dirty store window. Empty stores multiply. Abandoned and emasculated autos litter the streets and vacant lots. Marginal businesses come and go. Our private sector is not just demoralized; it's dying.

Not only were good businesses moving, so were the residents. The population of the Lower North Side had begun to decline more drastically than that of the city as a whole. (See Table II.)

By 1970 seventy per cent of all the residential units on the Lower North Side were in government-owned housing. (In 1930 the area did not contain a single unit of public housing.) In addition, another twenty per cent of the apartment units were occupied by families or individuals whose rents in privately owned housing were federally subsidized in one way or another. Only ten per cent of the families lived in housing without benefit of a federal subsidy. Even the Town and Gardens complex was primarily occupied by federally subsidized renters.

The racial make-up of the Lower North Side had also shifted. (See Table II.) In 1940 the area was eighty-five per cent white. Thirty years later in 1970, it had become eighty-nine per cent black, the overwhelming majority in households with very low incomes. White households still living on the Lower North Side occupied only the eastern edge along LaSalle Drive or the northeastern corner just south of North Avenue. The earlier optimism, generated decades earlier by the building of the Cabrini row houses and the Marshall Field Garden Apartments, had been banished by destitution and depopulation which had not been foreseen.

Did the Lower North Side really have a future in 1970? Or would it be written off as "dead real estate"? Why did Chicago's high-rise

housing for low-income families turn out to be an urban disaster —
worse perhaps than the Great Chicago Fire of 1871? The urban
cynics who visited the Lower North Side quickly reminded civic
optimists that the area which Zorbaugh had dubbed a "slum" in
1929 still deserved that epithet nearly forty years later.
Furthermore, the deterioration and dilapidation which had festered
at the area's center now began to spread outward block by block,
invading the better, residential sections which had endured at the
area's northern and eastern edges closer to Lake Michigan.

4

Counterattack

People don't live in cities. They live in
neighborhoods. Neighborhoods are the building
blocks of cities. If neighborhoods die, cities
die. —Monsignor Geno C. Baroni

In the 1960s North Avenue, the northern boundary of the Lower North Side, came to be known as a "Mason-Dixon line" separating middle class whites from low-income blacks. In the weekly *Reader,* Nancy Banks described this racial line as follows:

> North Avenue is one of the most strictly drawn and zealously guarded racial dividing lines in Chicago. To the north is the white, affluent neighborhood of Lincoln Park. To the south. . .is an enclave of black homeowners and renters. They are poor people, for the most part, and their homes are run-down versions of the quaint two flats and frame cottages that have become so fashionable farther north. Nobody seems to have a name for this neighborhood; Lincoln Parkers simply refer to it as "below North Avenue."

For a dozen decades the housing blight and desolating poverty which had pockmarked the Lower North Side had been safely quarantined within its boundaries. Or so it seemed. The 1950s and 1960s, however, upset the sense of security. The slum clearance which had paved the way for Marshall Field Garden Apartments and later for Cabrini-Green Homes produced unintended consequences. Slum buildings could be demolished. But what then happened to the families occupying these dilapidated and dangerous houses? Where did families overwhelmed with alcoholism, drug abuse, juvenile delinquency or repeated pregnancies among unwed teen-agers go? Where did households struggling with unemployability, single parentage or mental and physical handicaps go? Often to another building within walking distance. Frequently, blight and over-crowding accompanied the travelers to their new homes, breeding a new slum or worsening an older one.

As Lower North Side residents relocated in the 1950s and 1960s, commercial and industrial development along the Chicago River to the south and west served as man-made barriers to the residential dilapidation and deterioration. No such moat protected the Lincoln Park or Gold Coast communities. Hence, many of the Lower North Side's displaced persons fled there, together with newcomers from the South and from Puerto Rico. In the postwar decades, the virulent housing blight spread north and east. It threatened the established and affluent communities of Lincoln Park and the Gold Coast. Both were regarded as choice Chicago neighborhoods, with-in strolling distance of Lake Michigan and its parks and beaches.

Urban Renewal Arrives

To safeguard Lincoln Park and the Gold Coast from the on-slaught of inner city blight, City Hall declared war in the early 1960s. With federal funds and the wholehearted endorsement of most community leaders, three Department of Urban Renewal projects, two immediately east of Cabrini-Green and the third north of the Lower North Side in the Lincoln Park community, defined a new urban battleground. Arthur Rubloff, the real estate patriarch who was to develop the largest residential complex in the area, summed up the prevailing opinion:

> We don't have the strength in the neighborhoods around the central city. They're decayed and the central business district can't survive without that backup.

In response, the City government deployed its urban renewal legions to step up the enforcement of building and zoning codes, to "deconvert" larger apartments which had been cut up into kitchen-ettes and to demolish substandard buildings so that the valuable land could be resold. To whom? To developers ready to erect high rises and townhouses for the middle class. Putting that land to its highest and best use would mean larger tax revenues.

In the first urban renewal project, the City undertook the clearing of a ribbon of land, running north and south, on the east side of

LaSalle Drive. This narrow strip, just across the street from the Lower North Side, was a block wide and nearly a half-mile long. Businesses and residences, some in good condition and others badly deteriorated, were torn down. The now vacant twenty-two acre tract was sold to a single developer, Arthur Rubloff. By the 1970s he had erected 2,600 apartments in high rises, townhouses and atrium buildings for middle-income and two-earner families. Rubloff named his development after Carl Sandburg, one of Chicago's best known poets and a former resident of the area. When Sandburg returned from North Carolina to visit Carl Sandburg Village, he chuckled with pleasure: "Never did I believe that an old Swede like me would have his name identified with such a major project."

The residential and commercial deterioration creeping east from the Lower North Side had been blocked. A buffer zone was now in place. In 1970 the City's Department of Urban Renewal staff hailed Carl Sandburg Village as a great victory. The Gold Coast and North Michigan Avenue had been saved. Increased revenues from property taxes delighted City officials trying to balance the municipal budget.

The celebration was not unanimous. Critics pointed out that the chief beneficiaries of the publicly sponsored project were the city's lakefront gentry. Why were scarce federal dollars, they asked, not being used to rescue the city's poor families from substandard housing? But the roaring public acclaim that greeted Carl Sandburg Village drowned out the scattered voices of protest.

The second urban renewal project targeted the Lincoln Park community. [A third urban renewal project is discussed in Chapter 11.] This was the predominantly residential community adjoining the Lower North Side on the north, fronting on Lake Michigan and lying just northwest of Carl Sandburg Village. The stated purpose of the Lincoln Park project was "to create a highly desirable, close-in urban environment." What was to be done? Urban renewal troops would stimulate the private rehabilitation of housing, make land available for new residential construction and encourage neighborhood revitalization.

How was this to be done? By strictly enforcing building codes, providing low-cost loans to rehabilitate properties, demolishing substandard buildings and relocating the families and businesses, closing down a broad diagonal street and transforming it into a park and mall, and widening North Avenue, the main east and west commercial street. It was also to be done by allowing local educational and medical institutions to expand their facilities and services; by working with the Chicago Board of Education to upgrade the quality of local elementary and secondary schools; and by building low-rise townhouses to create a Lincoln Park community predominantly occupied by home owners.

Priority was given to family housing, acres of new neighborhood parks, new supermarkets and the rehabilitation of solidly constructed buildings. The area's proximity to Michigan Avenue and downtown, along with "pro-active" leadership from the City's Department of Urban Renewal and cooperative community leaders, produced a second successful project by the early 1970s. Michael Serritella, past president of the Old Town Chamber of Commerce, described his neighboring Lincoln Park community as

> an area that has been turned around, coming back to a more stable resting place. No longer is it a community in transition. It's the fashionable place in Chicago to own a home — if you can afford townhouses costing $150,000 and higher.

Alan Sorkin, a developer of townhouses at the southern edge of Lincoln Park, reminisced:

> Fifteen to twenty years ago, a frequently asked question was: "Why do you live in the city?" Today the question often asked is, "Why do you live in the suburbs?". . . .the beauty of Lincoln Park and Lake Michigan have convinced many suburban commuters that there is more to life than clogged expressways, car pools and train schedules.

The counterattack on urban blight had finally prevailed, with leadership coming from the federal and local governments and cheers from the middle class living near Michigan Avenue or in the Lincoln Park community.

The success of the City's battle against blight in the communities next to the Lower North Side was retold everywhere. Nelson Forrest, executive director of the Greater North Michigan Avenue Association called Carl Sandburg Village, whose rental apartments had been converted into condominiums, "the most successful urban renewal project in the United States." Cabrini-Green no longer seemed to becloud downtown's view of the Lower North Side.

Old and New Realities

This new optimism, however, was short-lived. It ended abruptly on July 17, 1970, when two police officers were killed by a hail of bullets from a nineteen-story high rise in Cabrini-Green Homes. A sniper had felled the policemen, James Severin and Anthony Rizzato, while on duty. What most residents of the Lower North Side had always suspected was now found to be true. A Cabrini-Green resident, one of the first to move into a row house back in the 1940s and still there, expressed the prevailing sentiment forcefully:

> The cover-up is over. The whole world now knows that something is wrong in Cabrini-Green and that no magic wand will make our trouble go away.
>
> Sure, residents are at fault. Didn't they pull the trigger that gunned down the policemen? But the system is just as bad. How are you going to maintain law and order when gangs roam the corridors, control the elevators, and force younger kids to join up? How are you going to have a good life when you pack hundreds of families with thousands of fatherless youngsters into high-rise monstrosities?

The postwar optimism, which led civic leaders to believe that public housing projects would salvage the city's neighborhoods by providing decent housing for low-income, upwardly mobile families, came to a disastrous end.

The unrelenting ills of the Cabrini-Green housing project had been exposed. Downtown Chicago's political and financial establishment could no longer pretend that Cabrini-Green was hidden from view — behind the Merchandise Mart.

The City As Slumlord

Furthermore, a near revolutionary shift had taken place in residential proprietorship. For most of the 19th and 20th centuries, outsiders had stigmatized the Lower North Side's housing as slum. Its residents, however, had another opinion. A grandmother, now living in a working class suburb of Chicago, reflected on her youth:

> We were married in St. Philip Benizi Church, two blocks east of Montgomery Ward's. That's where I grew up. After the wedding we moved to Melrose Park. Not long afterwards they tore down St. Philip's. It was only then that my friends reminded me that I had been raised in a *slum*. That was news to me. My memories are

warm, enriching and romantic. I only hope that my children and grandchildren are as happy growing up in suburban Melrose Park as I was in Chicago's "Little Sicily."

The all-important difference was that the earlier slums — going back to the 1840s — had been privately owned and operated. Their landlords lived on the premises or next door. Those frame houses and substandard family tenements were early forms of private enterprise. On the other hand, large public housing projects discouraged private enterprise and small business. The heart of the Lower North Side had been converted into a gigantic public housing project managed by a single government agency, thanks to a continuing subsidy from the federal government. Unwittingly and unwillingly, the Chicago Housing Authority had become the biggest slumlord on the Lower North Side. That fact confounded both amateur reformers and professional planners.

Urban developers differentiate the *environment* of a given place (the physical, political and economic influences from outside) from the *conditions* of the site itself, (the forces emanating from within). When urban communities are under siege or deteriorating, they single out, rightly or wrongly, an outside enemy to blame. Their Goliath may be urban renewal, the threat of racial change, a thundering new expressway, poor enforcement of fire and building codes, lax police surveillance or indifferent elected officials. On the Lower North Side, however, the key obstacle to neighborhood revival had become the condition of the site itself. The "enemy within" was Cabrini-Green, one of the best known public housing projects in the United States.

When a neighborhood contains a thousand or more individual property owners, generalizations about the quality of life come slowly and cautiously. When, however, most of the housing is under single ownership, sweeping statements flow easily and carelessly. Ever since the 1950s, the press, radio and television have not hesitated to remind Cabrini-Green residents that the place they call home is a slum. In an unprecedented way, the mass media has shaped the image of the Cabrini-Green neighborhood as much as the residents themselves.

In the 1970s, there was new significance to the "slum" in *The Gold Coast and the Slum*. That social and economic riddle had now

become a *political* question as well. How ably would urban reformers negotiate with landlords who were municipal bureaucrats?
Would government proprietors tolerate the presence of unrelenting
poverty beyond the year 2000, as private landlords had in the previous century? How long would Cabrini-Green skyscrapers remain as
the housing of last resort for households headed by unwed mothers
with small children on public assistance? Would the government-
owned high rises still be there in the year 2000? What would be the
ultimate impact of Cabrini-Green upon the Lower North Side?

   These questions can be answered only by weighing the future of
the Near North Side, the larger community area which includes both
the Lower North Side and the Gold Coast lakefront section. The
Lower North Side is not an island separated from mainland Chicago
but is closely linked to Lake Michigan's Gold Coast area and to
Chicago's downtown. Their proximity to each other welds together
their futures.

5

A Lost Identity

Chicago is the great American city. . . .
Perhaps it is the last of the great
American cities. —Norman Mailer

As far as Chicago's mapmakers are concerned, the Lower North Side, at least by that name, is unknown territory. It cannot be found on maps produced by the City's planning department or in the many plans generated by downtown business leaders. But there is a Lower North Side for two community organizations which represent its residents and institutions. Both the Near North Community Organization and the Neighborhood Institutional Advisory Council identify the Lower North Side as their turf and use its boundaries to define their sphere of influence.

'Lower North': Past and Present

Prior to 1930, however, that area had more often been called "Lower North" or the "Lower North Community." For example, in the wake of the national unity forged by World War I, a membership organization was formed in 1919 to unite the area's wealthier easterners with its poorer westerners. That civic association was called the Lower North Community Council. As the years went by, the Council became less of a membership-based community organization and more of a social welfare agency. Eventually, its funding and leadership came from the lakefront elite who supported "uplift" programs for their western neighbors in "Little Italy." The Council's inability to survive as a bona fide community organization with a broadly based membership prompted Zorbaugh to

41

investigate the community. He documented the area's social and economic cleavage in his book.

The paternalistic turn taken by the Lower North Community Council in the middle 1920s explains why vestiges of the Lower North name remain to this day only within the western sector — away from the Gold Coast. There still is, for example, a Lower North Center located in the heart of Cabrini-Green. Today the Center aids public housing tenants as it once served the families of Little Italy. The Center, a descendant of the Lower North Community Council, is no longer managed by civic-minded women from the Gold Coast, but by Chicago Youth Centers, a private city-wide agency.

In 1977 the Center published a forty-eight page directory listing the institutions, schools, churches, and other agencies providing services "within the Lower North Side," i.e. the area west of LaSalle Drive. Only two of the listings had "Lower North" in their titles. Needless to say, none of these social agencies is located near the Gold Coast. Other traces of a Lower North Side community are difficult to unearth. The *Chicago Telephone Directory,* for example, does not carry a single listing under "Lower North." There is little public consciousness of a Lower North Side presence.

The "Lower North Side" name may not be well known, but the terrain which the name designates is. It is home, for example, to the Merchandise Mart, Montgomery Ward & Company and the Moody Bible Institute, each of which has earned a national and, in some cases, an international reputation for serving a world-wide network.

The area described thus far as the "Lower North Side" is better known today as the western section of the Near North Side, the name given to a larger community which also embraces Chicago's Gold Coast and nearby lakefront.

From where did the name "Near North Side" come? In the early 1930s university professors, seeking the identity of Chicago's many communities and lively neighborhoods, gave that name to the area west of Lake Michigan and immediately north of the Chicago River. That distinguished team of social scientists at the University of Chicago researched the city, divided it into seventy-five community areas — now grown to seventy-seven — and began compiling census information on these areas. On their Chicago map, they designated the area immediately north of the Chicago River and east of its North Branch as the Near North Side, or Community Area #8. (See map.) Though never stamped with official approval by the City's planning department, the University of Chicago map came to be the accepted way of locating and naming Chicago's communities and provided residents of each area with a sense of identity and belonging.

The most recent *Local Community Fact Book* sets out the criteria which the University of Chicago professors used to draw the community boundaries. They took into account

> (1) the settlement, growth and history of the area; (2) local identi- fication with the area; (3) the local trade area; (4) distribution of membership in local institutions; and (5) natural and artificial barriers such as the Chicago River and its branches, railroad lines, local transportation systems, and parks and boulevards.

In sorting out the original seventy-five Chicago communities, the scholarly mapmakers recognized that the modern metropolis was a "city of cities," a "mosaic of little worlds" and an "aggregate of local communities," each different from the other. The Near North Side was one of those "little worlds" in the big and booming Chicago of the 1930s.

Identifying the Near North Side

Unlike the Lower North Side, the "Near North Side" name, containing as it does the "Lower North" slum and the lakefront Gold Coast, is well entrenched in public usage. The *Chicago Telephone Directory,* for example, carries thirty listings under the "Near North" heading.

The question no longer arises about the Near North Side name but about the borders established in 1930. Do these venerable boundaries continue to outline a recognizable community? The University of Chicago demographers offered an equivocal answer. They fully appreciated that Chicago had not yet matured as a city, that it retained its dynamic and changing character. Hence, five decades later, the authors of the latest *Local Community Fact Book,* cautioned their readers:

> Community areas at the present time are best regarded as statisti- cal units for the analysis of varying conditions within the City of Chicago at a given time, and for studying changes over time in

conditions within local communities. . . . The community areas, for which Chicago statistics have been compiled since 1930, not only serve this purpose admirably, but they remain, in many cases, meaningful local communities.

Is the Near North Side, known as Community Area #8, to be regarded solely as a statistical unit? Or do its community boundaries still apply? Do its 300 city blocks indeed circumscribe a viable and "meaningful" local community that would be recognized as such in the 1990s?

The Near North Side is one of the few community areas whose boundaries are mostly defined by nature. On three sides, the Near North Side's boundaries coincide with those of the Lower North Side, but on the east the border extends to Lake Michigan, not LaSalle Drive. The Near North Side is "near north" in relation to the commercial, business, financial and governmental center immediately south of the river.

The Near North Side is held together by four business streets running east and west. The most important of these, choked day and evening with vehicular traffic, is Chicago Avenue. As the main avenue of commerce between the eastern and western sections, Chicago Avenue begins on the east at Lake Michigan, runs through the entire area and crosses over the North Branch of the Chicago River westward to the city limits and beyond. Two of the Near North Side's most conspicuous landmarks can be found along the Chicago Avenue axis. At the western edge, the highly visible bronze statue of "The Spirit of Progress" stands on top of a Montgomery Ward building. In the other direction the old Water Tower stands at the intersection of Michigan Avenue. Built in 1867 and famous for having survived the great fire of 1871, the Water Tower overlooks Chicago's most fashionable shopping and hotel district. Were the eastern sector of the Near North Side ever to shed its constricting Gold Coast name, it would likely come to be known as the Water Tower area. The Spirit of Progress and the Water Tower are fragments of the past. Yet, as history-laden landmarks, they accent the Near North Side's distinctively urban character.

Partitioning the Near North Side

The natural configuration of the Near North Side's borders and its geographic compactness would seem to ensure the presence of a genuine and united community. The welfare not only of Community Area #8 but of the city itself would best be served by keeping the area intact for political, service, educational and other municipal functions. The boundaries of the Near North Side, however, are not the same as those of any political or service district. The entire Near North Side is lost in several larger districts:

- the Fourth and Eighth Illinois Legislative Districts which send, respectively, a senator and a representative to the Illinois General Assembly in Springfield;

- the Chicago Board of Education's North High School District and its Elementary School District #3; the Eighteenth Police District (better known as the Chicago Avenue District); the "region one service area" of the Illinois Department of Mental Health; the Youth Service Planning Area #72 of the Illinois Department of Children and Family Services; the Chicago Cable Franchise Area #1, one of the City's five service areas for cable television; and

- Vicariate V, one of the twelve regions into which the Catholic Archdiocese (covering Cook and Lake Counties in Illinois) is divided.

In each of the service areas above, the district boundaries do not split up the Near North Side; they simply make it a part of some larger district.

Other district boundaries, however, do divide the Near North Side, thus disjointing its governmental and political loyalties:

- Its population is shared between the 42nd and 43rd Wards and between the 7th and 9th Congressional Districts.

- While the Near North Side has four postal zip codes (60610, 60611, 60654 and 60671) of its own, it is also part of a fifth (60622).

- For planning purposes, City Hall arranges Chicago into twelve planning districts and in doing so splits up the Near North Side. Its northern section (including Cabrini-Green) is attached to "North Neighborhood-Planning District #V," while the remaining portion falls under the jurisdiction of a "Central Area Planning District."

- The Chicago Department of Health slices the Near North Side through the middle, along Chicago Avenue. Each half is assigned to a larger and different "community" which is served by its own "community-based mental health center."

● To improve the industrial corridor along the North Branch of
the Chicago River, the Local Economic and Employment
Development Council was organized in the 1980s. The
Council takes in much of the Near North Side's western
section, including Cabrini-Green. That same section is also
part of Enterprise Zone 4, a larger area designated by the City
and State as "economically depressed."

An Area of Diversity

The Near North Side's heterogeneity is legendary. The voters in
the state legislative district which includes the Near North Side and
neighboring Lincoln Park are seventy-five per cent white. Jesse
White, the elected official who represents the area in the Illinois
General Assembly, is black. One U.S. Congressman is white; the
other is black; and the Illinois State Senator who represents the Near
North Side is white. None of the last three lives on the Near North
Side; they reside elsewhere in the larger legislative district which
each represents. In the hotly contested election for mayor of
Chicago in 1983, the Lower North Side voted a hundred to one for
the Democratic winner, Harold Washington. The Gold Coast section voted three to one for the loser, Bernard Epton, a Republican
who attracted a large number of normally Democratic voters. In a
high-rise building close to the lakefront, the residence of former
Democratic Mayor Jane Byrne, the occupants voted five to one for
Epton.

As it was in Zorbaugh's time five decades earlier, the Near North
Side remains a place of startling contrasts. It is the birthplace of
Poetry magazine and the home of *Playboy*. It holds the headquar-
ters of the Great Books Foundation and the site where that unique
American achievement, the mail order catalog, was perfected.
Three cathedrals, Annunciation (Greek Orthodox), Holy Name
(Roman Catholic) and St. James (Episcopal) grace the Near North
Side, along with twenty-one storefront churches. Chicago's historic
Washington Park and its "Bughouse Square," the Museum of Con-
temporary Art, Newberry Library, the downtown campuses of
Loyola and Northwestern Universities, the national offices of the
American Medical Association, the American Bar Association,
American Dental Association, the National Congress of Parents
and Teachers and the local offices of the AFL-CIO's Chicago
Federation of Labor are all here.

An Area Divided

It takes ten minutes to walk from Cabrini-Green Homes to the Gold Coast. On certain days of the year, the John Hancock Center, located on Michigan Avenue and one of the world's tallest buildings, can cast its early morning shadow on Cabrini-Green Homes.

The eastern and western sections of the Near North Side are physically close, but the social distance is immense. In 1929, after he discovered the schizophrenic world of the Near North Side, Zorbaugh described the paradox in *The Gold Coast and the Slum.* The Near North Side, he wrote, is an urban turf deeply divided into

> an area of high light and shadow, of vivid contrasts — contrasts not only between the old and the new, between the native and the foreign, but between wealth and poverty, vice and respectability, the conventional and the bohemian, luxury and toil.

When Cabrini-Green is juxtaposed in the 1980s with Lake Michigan's Gold Coast where Chicago's choicest real estate can be found, the contrast is shocking. The household income in Cabrini-Green averages about $5,000 annually. Along East Lake Shore Drive, family incomes of $400,000 a year are not uncommon. Rents in Cabrini-Green average less than $1,000 a year; on East Lake Shore Drive rents run as high as $84,000 a year. The land value next to some sections of Cabrini-Green runs about $600 a front foot; at the north end of Michigan Avenue, near the lake, the land is valued at $50,000 a front foot.

More Contrasts

Although Cabrini-Green has replaced Little Italy, the Near North Side's split personality is still in public view. When the City of Chicago and downtown business leaders jointly unveiled a "Chicago 21" plan in 1973 to revive the central business district, the plan depicted the Near North Side as having within its boundaries

> some of the best and some of the worst conditions. . . .the Gold Coast with dynamic office and residential development, [exerts] a positive influence. North Michigan Avenue [has] quality shopping, hotels and offices. . . .

> At the opposite extreme of this spectrum is the Cabrini-Green public housing project and the surrounding residential area. Physical, economic and social problems pervade here, contributing to a high crime rate, instability and other chaotic conditions.

In 1984 a streetwise security guard, who watches over the tenants of his luxurious high rise near Lake Michigan, described the incongruities:

> You want to know the real difference between the Lower North Side and the Gold Coast? I'll tell you. Here on the Gold Coast we debate the wisdom of allowing horse-driven carriages (rented at $20 a half-hour to tourists, honeymooners and other romantics) on our streets. We argue about traffic hazards and the size of the diapers worn by the horses.
>
> Over there, on the other side, the battle is over the stabling of the same horses. The people there are resisting the stinking and messy stables inflicted upon them. I don't blame them. Right now they're stuck with two stables, with others to come. The Gold Coast would never tolerate a barnyard near Lake Michigan. You can bet on that.

The security guard was not finished. He quickly added:

> Where do pickpockets operate? Where do the burglaries take place? Along the Gold Coast and its neighboring streets. The thieves don't live here, but it's here that they make their living.
>
> Once the city banned street musicians, magicians and mimes. Now that the law sides with street performers, they can legally fiddle their tunes, dance their jigs, and sing their melodies. But you won't find any of them in Cabrini-Green. There's no money in it for them. Anyhow, they might get mugged. On our side, they're fingered as panhandlers. But the Arts Council hails them as talented musicians and actors. Who's right?
>
> At night, our sidewalks are jammed with life and people. Over there, the streets are dead and dangerous. At all hours of the evening, you'll find more Cabrini-Green people on our streets than theirs.

In 1983 the editor of the weekly *Near North News,* voicing an editorial opinion, pointed out still another difference between the two sections. It is well known, he said, that:

> All forms of gambling prey on the poor and the uninformed. Those who are already down-and-out are the ones most likely to take a flyer on a gamble where the odds are flagrantly stacked against them. The well-to-do and the well-educated may gamble on such things as the commodities market, but they tend to do it on the basis of more or less careful study and only with the money they can afford to lose.

That's what makes official gambling all the worse. We don't see people who live on Lake Shore Drive lined up buying state lottery tickets. We do see people who live in Cabrini-Green desperately trying to buck the odds.

There is reason to believe that the entire Illinois lottery system is a hoax. . . .a rip off. But we do feel sorry for the innocents who continue to spend their scarce cash on such get-rich-quick schemes.

The two areas are racially different. In 1980 residents of the Lower North Side were ninety per cent black, its population having shrunk steadily since 1940. The population of the Gold Coast, however, was about ninety-five per cent white in 1980, without much change numerically over the same period. (See Table III in Chapter 10.) A teacher in a Cabrini-Green school pointed out the overriding distinction between the two populations:

The great majority of the households close to the lakefront are childless. The kids are *here*, near Cabrini-Green and Town and Gardens. If you see a youngster on any of the streets near the Gold Coast, you can assume that the kid is a visitor.

Most of the elementary and secondary schools in the Cabrini-Green section are public. (One Catholic elementary school is still here.)

Nearer to the lakefront, the educational scene changes. Most of the schools are privately sponsored and enroll students city-wide. Ogden, the only public elementary school, can serve a population of 50,000!

A pastor, whose parishioners live in Cabrini-Green, accented another difference:

You want to know what divides us from the Gold Coast? They call their section the Gold Coast. Isn't that enough? They live in Chicago's front yard facing Lake Michigan. We're its back yard. Our common alley is the winding and polluted Chicago River near which I live. The cathedrals are located not here but over there — nearer the lake.

Divided Loyalties

Within the Lower North Side itself there is little willingness to identify with any area cut off at, and lying west of, LaSalle Drive. The push is in the other direction. Lower North Side businesses, school principals and residents actively want to associate themselves

— under the "Near North Side" umbrella — with the prosperity, visibility and prestige of the Gold Coast and its North Michigan Avenue shopping district. As a matter of fact, church and community leaders, including Cabrini-Green residents, strongly oppose any name other than Near North Side. An active member of the Cabrini-Green Local Advisory Council summed up the point-of-view of most public housing tenants:

> We are trying to upgrade our neighborhood. Do you think that "Lower North Side" does anything for our image? The "Near North Side" does something for us. It has the pizazz we want. That's where our future is.

That optic is also shared by the oldest community organization on the Lower North Side: the Neighborhood Institutional Advisory Council. Founded in 1958, it brings together the staffs of religious and welfare institutions to serve better the residents of the Lower North Side. When Council leaders in 1984 published a roster of agencies serving the Lower North Side, they called it the *Near North Directory*. Yet, the map it contained was of the Lower North Side, the area west of LaSalle Drive.

In the 1970s when another community group was organized to rejuvenate the Lower North Side, the organizers from local churches and Cabrini-Green insisted that it be called the Near North Community Organization. James B. White, the first full-time executive director of the NNCO, underlined the importance of the "Near North" part of the name:

> One of the reasons why our community has outstanding. . .potential for revitalization is its location. [We are] strategically located just north of the Loop, with easy access to the city's cultural, economic and social heart. Furthermore, to the east is Chicago's famous Gold Coast area, where a mix of luxury housing, exclusive shopping facilities and restaurants have made the area Chicago's most valuable real estate.

The NNCO leaders wanted the best of both worlds. They organized themselves to rejuvenate the Lower North Side where they lived or worked, but they also sought to hitch their future to the success and resources of the Gold Coast. By adopting the "Near North" name, they hoped to gain direct access to the lakefront towards the east. A Cabrini-Green resident who was preparing to move out of her high rise pinpointed the advantage she saw in the "Near North" connection:

> I don't mind associating with the rich folks near the lake. I hope some of their glitter rubs off — on me. They may not want to mix with me and my kin. I know that. And that's not what I want.

> What I and my children want is a chance to move up a rung or two on the ladder. While the foot of the ladder is here, the top rests somewhere else — in some place more like what's going on near the lakefront.

Those who live on the Lower North Side clearly prefer to be known as Near North Siders. Would the affluent Gold Coast honor their wish?

The View From the Gold Coast

Residents of the lakefront Gold Coast area see themselves comfortably settled in their own enclave near the lakefront. Here they feel safe and secure. That isolationist stance is taken by an advertising executive whose offices overlook North Michigan Avenue and its environs:

> We can make it on our own. If the police do their job and if our private security systems work, we won't have to worry about pickpockets, purse snatchers and muggers from the west, who can give us trouble.

Entranced by bounding prosperity and unprecedented economic growth, merchants and residents of the Gold Coast have little problem with the "Near North Side" designation. In their imagination, they regard LaSalle Drive as their western border. They are content as long as they — and the Near North Side — are not identified with the western part, the Lower North Side. A room clerk at a Gold Coast hotel stressed this point:

> For the people who use this hotel, Cabrini-Green is foreign country, an urban jungle to be visited in an armored car, to be explored but not to be settled. It's inconvenient to have that section part of the Near North Side. As long as nobody notices the connection, we're okay. Had they drawn our western boundary somewhere near LaSalle Drive it would have been perfect.

Alliances Spurned

On the Lower North Side, looking out from the twenty-sixth floor of their newest building, Montgomery Ward executives saw, and were delighted at, the amazing growth of the lakefront section. However, they were distressed by the reluctance of that lakefront sector, a mile to the east, to join hands with its western counterpart where Ward's headquarters is located. Montgomery Ward had joined the Greater North Michigan Avenue Association (GNMAA), which primarily represented the commercial, financial and residential interests of the lakefront area. With periodic prodding from Montgomery Ward, the GNMAA resuscitated its Western Sector Council in order to demonstrate its concern for the welfare and redevelopment of the Lower North Side. Inevitably, the GNMAA's attention was short-lived, mesmerized as it was by the astonishing commercial development along both sides of the so-called "Magnificent Mile," the name given to North Michigan Avenue by real estate, public relations and advertising tycoons. To the consternation of Ward's executives, the Western Sector Council never made good as a viable organization.

Ward's offices front on Chicago Avenue. Why did this east/west avenue of commerce fail to unite the eastern and western sectors of the Near North Side? A police officer explains:

> Social intercourse between the Lower North Side and the Gold Coast is by telephone, the U.S. mail or the computer; by delivery truck, public buses or taxi cabs. Except for what the churches do, one-to-one contact seldom occurs, except for purse snatchings.

The Downtown Connection

Conversely, Michigan Avenue did succeed in connecting the Gold Coast lakefront to the central business district downtown. This north and south connection was not always there. It was late in coming.

The city's elevated transit system, completed in 1897, looped its tracks around Chicago's downtown business section. That steel girdle, as Harold M. Mayer and Richard C. Wade noted in *Chicago: Growth of a Metropolis,* had "unmistakably defined the core of Chicago's central business district and identified desirable and prestigious locations." The Loop eventually encompassed City Hall, the State of Illinois building, federal government offices, the largest banks, the city's financial district on LaSalle Street, the major hotels and the most fashionable department stores. The intersection of State and Madison Streets was touted as "the busiest corner in the world."

In succeeding decades the downtown business district slowly extended its domain beyond the Loop of elevated transit tracks to the river on the west and north, to Michigan Avenue on the east and to the railroad yards on the south. The Loop business district prospered because it was the hub of an incomparable concentration of rail, vehicular and waterway transportation within the city and from out of state. The Loop remained the heart of Chicago until the wide, two-level Michigan Avenue bridge was opened in 1920. With the advent of the automobile, that bridge spurred the rapid development of new skyscrapers, luxury hotels, swank offices and elegant shops on Michigan Avenue north of the river.

By the 1960s, four decades later, it began to look as if the "old downtown" on State Street south of the Chicago River would be replaced by the "new downtown" being established via the Michigan Avenue bridge north of the river. Accordingly, City Hall planners, downtown retailers and the city's powerful bankers became preoccupied with the economic future of their historic downtown business district. They watched, with increasing concern, the spectacular retail and commercial expansion along North Michigan Avenue and the appearance of hotels and restaurants north of the river, as those downtown were being demolished.

The civic and business leaders also lamented the departure of many corporate headquarters to suburban sites; the opening of giant shopping centers in the suburban ring around the city; the decline of downtown movie houses and live theater; the racially changing patronage of downtown's retail establishments and entertainment houses; and the decreasing presence of a white middle class in the Loop during the evening and weekend hours. Was Chicago's downtown no longer viable? Would it go the way of the central business districts in Detroit, Cleveland, Newark, St. Louis, Washington and elsewhere?

Distracted by such problems, downtown Chicago's civic leaders sought alliances that would strengthen their own economy, giving top priority to the revitalization of the central business district and leaving the Lower North Side to sink or swim on its own. While the *Chicago 21* plan of 1973 devoted several pages to the upgrading of the Lower North Side, the plan's real agenda was the health and welfare of the central business district. With the help of City Hall the downtown business establishment steered attention to its nearby "competitor," the Gold Coast and its lakefront. This section was enjoying a retailing, banking, business and residential boom. By 1986, post-war investment in new building had passed the $10 billion mark. Sales and customer traffic along the North Michigan Avenue corridor surged year after year, while downtown retail sales dropped. Before long, maps of Chicago's central business district began to include the "new downtown" north of the river. North Michigan Avenue had become the northern anchor of the city's central business district. In 1983 Arnie Matanky, editor of *Near North News,* could safely remind his readers that once there had been

> days in the dim past when Michigan Avenue and State Street were mortal enemies, each convinced that the other was trying to destroy its prosperity. Now downtown and the Near North Side are for all practical purposes one community.

The Isolation of the Lower North Side

Both the Gold Coast and downtown leadership had disowned the Lower North Side in the early 1970s. On the one hand, the Lower North Side was seen as an unwanted stepchild in the Near North Side family. On the other hand, the central business district regarded it as a poor and distant cousin whose courtship of City Hall had gone unrequited.

Despite these rejections the Lower North Side continued its search for allies who would help revitalize it. But would the Lower North Side flounder, trying to survive as a community on its own? Or would its future lie instead under the canopy of the Near North Side? Would the Gold Coast and the slum eventually come together as one community? The answer to these questions is closely tied to the destiny of the gigantic public housing project which dominates every discussion of the Lower North Side's future.

For the enigma is the century-old persistence of poverty on the Lower North Side, centered today in the Cabrini-Green public housing project. Since the Lower North Side is no longer a port of entry for newcomers to the city, who or what will eventually replace Cabrini-Green as it had earlier displaced Little Italy?

6

Cabrini-Green: Who's in Charge?

*The trouble with half-truths. . .is the
other half.* —Kenneth Boulding, *Beasts
Ballads and Bouldingisms*

What is Cabrini-Green? It is the most publicized of Chicago's
twenty-five high-rise public housing projects for families, owned
and operated by the Chicago Housing Authority*. In the middle
1980s some 13,500 persons — possibly many more — call Cabrini-
Green their home.

For most Chicagoans, Cabrini-Green is a foreign country, a place
they have never visited. They have to imagine what it is like to live
there. They seldom see or experience it personally. Unlike other
public housing projects in Chicago, Cabrini-Green cannot be seen
from the major expressways. Chicagoans read about Cabrini-Green
the way they scan news reports from abroad or view foreign events
via a television satellite. What they eventually know comes from
these newspaper headlines or from sensational scenes of violence on
local television. They would never enter Cabrini-Green, visit a
family there or drive by unless they worked nearby.

It is easy to describe Cabrini-Green in the language of brick and
mortar. Its seventy-eight buildings contain 3,600 apartments built at
a cost of $61 million, though the replacement cost is estimated at
more than $200 million. Cabrini-Green competes nationally with

---

*From this point on, the Chicago Housing Authority will be referred to as
the CHA, the three-letter name generally used by Chicagoans.

A nineteen-story high rise in Cabrini-Green

Montgomery Ward, the Moody Bible Institute, Oscar Mayer and the Merchandise Mart as the Lower North Side's best-known institution.

Cabrini-Green is the name given to the troika of housing developments covering seventy acres of potentially valuable and intensely urban turf located in the north central section of the Lower North Side. Frances Cabrini Homes (the row houses) was completed in 1943; the Cabrini Extension (fifteen red brick high rises) was occupied in 1958; and William Green Homes (eight gray concrete high rises) was finished in 1962. Two neighboring CHA high rises for the elderly, not part of Cabrini-Green, were occupied in 1965 and called Flannery Apartments; their occupants try not to be identified with Cabrini-Green even though their buildings fall under the jurisdiction of the manager of Cabrini-Green.

Architecturally speaking, the view of Cabrini-Green is deceptive. Early in 1980 twenty-five Chicagoans, all college graduates, were asked to identify an unmarked photograph of Cabrini-Green, taken from a downtown skyscraper. Not one identified the scene as Cabrini-Green, and *only one* dubbed it a public housing project. Viewed from a tourists' lookout atop Chicago's John Hancock Center or the Sears Tower, Cabrini-Green looks like any other large high-rise complex. From a distance, Cabrini-Green's towers resemble middle class, residential skyscrapers. Up close, however, Cabrini-Green's physical plant is visibly in need of massive repairs.

How does the CHA finance and manage Cabrini-Green? With money received from rents plus federal and City subsidies. As a municipal corporation organized in Illinois, CHA pays no property taxes. In the 1960s the CHA made a token donation of $1.8 million annually in lieu of taxes to the county. After the CHA became a losing undertaking in the 1970s, this payment stopped. Cabrini-Green seldom balances its budget. Its annual operating deficit goes beyond $2 million. Cabrini-Green staggers under a per capita maintenance cost higher than that of any other public housing project in the city.

Cabrini-Green apartments range in size from one to five bedrooms. For all apartments regardless of size the average rent is $85 a month, which usually represents thirty per cent of a household's adjusted gross income. Income limits for admission vary according to the size of the family: $19,600 annually for a family of four and

$22,000 for a family of six. Rarely, if ever, does a family move in whose income is that high, unless it is a household with ten or more children. In 1986 the average income of a Cabrini-Green household was around $5,000 a year.

A 'City' of Women and Children

Who lives in Cabrini-Green today? The answer to this question is neither simple nor easy to determine. The residents are black and disproportionately young; they belong to extremely poor households which suffer from a dramatic shortage of adults, particularly men. The CHA's official answers about occupancy are neat and precise. In 1966 the Cabrini-Green manager reported a peak population of 20,000 residents, seventy per cent of whom were under seventeen years of age. By 1981, however, the CHA reported that only 13,500 persons occupied Cabrini-Green. Sixty-six per cent were minors, and the rest were adults who were twenty-one and older. Ninety-one per cent of the families with children were headed by women. The size of the average household was 3.8 persons. Only those whose names appeared in a CHA lease were counted as official CHA residents.

The drop in the *official* count of tenants can be explained. It mirrors the changes in birth rates in society as a whole. In 1966 the majority of the households had two parents and the average family size was 5.6. Since then, falling birth rates, smaller families, younger and unwed mothers, absent fathers and disappearing teen-agers brought the average family size down to 3.8 by the early 1980s.

Cabrini-Green is still a child-centered housing project, dominated by preschool and elementary school children. In recent years, there are noticeably fewer adolescents than one might expect. Why? There is bad news and good news. Some teen-agers wind up in jail, at the morgue or in mental institutions, while others join the city's underworld of gangs, crime, drugs and prostitution. On the other hand, many teen-agers go to live with relatives or friends elsewhere in order to escape the gangs and brutal violence. These Cabrini-Green youngsters are highly motivated and upwardly mobile, and many leave with the encouragement and assistance of their mothers.

Also contributing to Cabrini-Green's depopulation is its reputation for violence. Vacancies became abnormally high after the slaying of two policemen in 1970. More apartments remained empty because they needed major repair, while still others were converted to such nonresidential uses as day care centers or offices. Consequently, the official Cabrini-Green population fell from a peak of 20,000 in 1966 to 13,500 in 1981. The official count has not changed since then.

Official and Unofficial Counts — 1981, For Example

These occupancy figures conceal a paradox. While the official population has declined steadily since the late 1960s, the unofficial occupancy has risen each year. The unofficial statistics tell an incredible story. In 1981 the *Chicago Tribune* reported that:

> Cabrini now has. . .an unregistered population of as many as 6,000. Six hundred of those residents are active gang members and sympathizers, the police said.

That is not all. In the same year John Wells wrote in the *Inland Architect* that Cabrini-Green is "a public housing project. . .where (officially) 13,500 blacks live and where there are more likely 22,000."

These estimates, or guesses, seem conservative when compared to those quoted by Renault Robinson, a CHA board member in 1981 and subsequently its chairman. In a statement that same year to the Illinois Advisory Committee to the U.S. Commission on Civil Rights, Robinson produced his own data. Speaking of CHA's city-wide population, he claimed that

> statistically we house 140,000 people. That's what we've got on paper. But in reality, it's about 300,000 because we have two and three families staying in one unit because they have nowhere to go.

If Robinson's own city-wide estimate of unregistered tenants were pro-rated among the various projects and applied specifically to Cabrini-Green, its total population, registered and unauthorized, would rise to 28,000.

How many residents does Cabrini-Green really house? How many are bona fide? How many are trespassers? The riddle remains unsolved. An experienced police sergeant on the Lower North Side added a pinch of realism to the CHA's statistical chowder:

> Don't trust those CHA figures. Of the original 3,600 Cabrini-Green apartments, nearly five hundred are unfit for human habitation. Add to this number those apartments that CHA cannot rent.

Robinson's estimates are far too high. Whatever their source, these hit-and-miss statistics telegraph a message: Cabrini-Green's management office has little honest-to-God information on who's who in most high-rise apartments. Unbelievable? But that's life in a project.

The policeman's insight was corroborated by an incident that also occurred in 1981 when Mayor Jane Byrne was sojourning in Cabrini-Green, on and off, for three weeks. Three City officials were scouting for another vacant apartment in one of the high rises. They were hunting for a clean, empty apartment which could be used temporarily by a Cabrini-Green family whose own unit was being fumigated to rid it of roaches, bedbugs and other vermin. One member of the trio was the CHA manager of Cabrini-Green. From his bulky file of vacancies he took three numbered keys. Arriving at the first apartment, with "vacant" stencilled on the door, the manager inserted the key. The lock would not open. He knocked on the door, and a pleasant female voice chimed from inside, "Who's there?" They then went to the second apartment, also with "vacant" stencilled on the door. This time the key did not even fit the lock. Again he rapped on the door, and a woman's voice came back, "Who's there?" His third key, however, did work. The "vacant" apartment was indeed empty of tenants, but occupied, wall to wall, by garbage and trash.

Nonplussed by the experience, the Cabrini-Green manager could not answer these questions from his two companions:

> How could two officially vacant apartments be occupied without the CHA's knowledge? Who had the locks changed so that the CHA's own keys would be useless? Was rent being paid? If so, to whom? Were the occupants registered voters? Did they vote on election day? Was the situation any different in the other high rises?

Illegal Tenants

The simple truth is that nobody, including the Cabrini-Green manager, really knows how many unregistered tenants live in Cabrini-Green. Those who guess that there are six thousand are more likely to be right than those who claim that there are fifteen thousand. Illegal homesteaders drift to the taller buildings which contain hundreds of vacant, boarded up or vandalized apartments.

Who, typically, are the unauthorized, unregistered tenants? They show up in different ways:

- Squatters take over an officially vacant apartment or they break into another apartment sealed off because it was unfit for human occupancy.

- Families evicted for failure to pay rent or for criminal violations, such a rape or drug peddling, move back into any vacant apartments whether habitable or not.

- Families move in with other families and share the rent without notifying the CHA. (One eviction by the sheriff's police involved ten occupants, but only two of the names were on the CHA lease.)

- Persons rent rooms from families living in four and five bedroom apartments.

- Gang leaders and other hoodlums muscle their way into apartments occupied by elderly persons and settle in. They intimidate anybody who would report them to the police.

- Nomadic fathers whose names rarely appear on a CHA lease come and go.

- Babies born to unwed teen-age girls are often entrusted to their new grandmothers.

Hundreds of ex-convicts move in. Most pay no rent to anyone. Illinois legislator Jesse White, a Lower North Side resident, explained how the system was exploited by these "undesirables":

> The state released a lot of offenders — paroled them out — because the prisons were getting overcrowded. They'd meet a guy in prison and say, "I have a girlfriend who lives in Cabrini-Green, and you can come live with us." Another guy would say, "I know a lady over there who has an apartment with four bedrooms," and they'd go over and tell her they'd like to rent one of her rooms and will give her $75 a month apiece; maybe she's paying $40. That's how we get a lot of our problems. Then there were the situations where they would intimidate people: "If you don't let him live here, we're gonna harm your family, do a job on your kid, slash your tires," etc. We even have problems with people who had to *pay* to go into buildings.

Weal and Woe

The metaphor that best catches life in Cabrini-Green is the roller coaster. Eventually the rampageous ride comes to an end — at the bottom of the slide. The Cabrini-Green roller coaster, however, is not an amusement ride. The life cycle in the project alternates between fear and excitement, weal and woe, shame and pride, terror and relief. Its human contradictions are graphically documented in these headlines taken from a decade of newspaper stories.

In 1974 the *Chicago Defender*'s headline announced, "Suspects sought in Cabrini-Green death." The story then read:

> The sun was bright and high overhead at about noon yesterday, the last day of Bessie Anderson's young life. She was sitting outside the door of her ground floor apartment in the Chicago Housing Authority's Cabrini-Green project. Bessie, 20, was looking after two young children playing in the grassy space between the sidewalk and the high-rise building at 624 W. Division Street. . . .
> A single stray bullet struck Bessie Anderson in the head, killing her. . . .Police say it is not unusual for a Cabrini-Green killing to take place in broad daylight and be witnessed by dozens of people. What is unusual is for witnesses to come forward with positive identifications.

A few months later the headline in the *Chicago Tribune* was, "Cops Target of Cabrini Sniper." The story said that:

> Investigating a common report of a "burglary in progress," six policemen became stuck in a disabled elevator in the Cabrini-Green Homes housing project. . .and then had to dodge a hail of sniper bullets as they left the cover of the building. The bullets shattered two windows in a squad car, but none of the policemen were wounded. . . .The 13th floor apartment at 1340 N. Larrabee St., where the burglary was reported, turned out to be unoccupied. The call apparently was a phony, said the sergeant.

In 1975, trying to fill vacant apartments, the CHA began advertising on Chicago Transit Authority elevated trains and distributed an eight-page brochure titled "Cabrini-Green is changing. . .and there's a lot that you don't know about the improvements." At the time the CHA claimed it had a city-wide waiting list of 9,000 families, but few could be persuaded to rent in Cabrini-Green.

In 1976 the editorial in the *Chicago Sun-Times*, "Sunlight at Cabrini-Green," said:

> Hopeful changes are being made in the lives of residents of the Cabrini-Green public housing project on the North Side. The changes are partial and gradual. But they are nevertheless important. . . .Cabrini-Green has come a long way since the early 1970s, when it was a hotbed of gang terrorism.

A year later in 1977, the *Chicago Defender*'s headline read, "CHA Project Getting Results at Cabrini." The following year a headline in the *Chicago Tribune* announced, "Cabrini-Green 'hopeless no longer': Government Investment Pays Off." The reporter continued:

> In the summer of 1970, two Chicago policemen were gunned down in a volley of sniper bullets as they walked their beat in the Cabrini-Green public housing development. The slayings spotlighted the sprawling, crime-ridden Near North Side project as an example of the failure of public housing.
>
> City officials, shocked by the deaths, had to make a choice: demolish Cabrini, or try to make it a liveable, viable family development. Eight years later, it's beginning to look like their decision to choose the latter alternative was the right one.

In 1979, however, the headlines began to change once again. The *Chicago Tribune* announced, "Cabrini-Green Area Thieves Prey on Women Drivers in Daylight." A feature story by Anne Keegan was headlined, "Daylight robbers find drivers easy pickings." In 1980, the familiar headline returned to the front page of the *Chicago Defender*, "Fears Haunt Cabrini-Green: Dynamite or Condo?"

But a year later, after Mayor Jane Byrne had spent several days in Cabrini-Green, Anne Keegan's newest article was headlined, "All Agree: Life is Better Now at Cabrini." In the *Chicago Tribune,* she wrote:

> Jane Byrne changed things at Cabrini-Green. Despite her vow, an elite place it will never be. A liveable place it has become. And that's all the tenants wanted in the first place.

A similar article appeared in the same year in the *Chicago Sun-Times*, "Cabrini-Green No Longer 'Hell on Earth'." The opening paragraph of the story read:

> Cabrini-Green, in the six months since Mayor Byrne put it in the spotlight, hasn't become the Gold Coast, but it's no longer the hellish place it used to be. . . .
>
> Police heavy-handedness in dealing with loiterers and others also has been criticized. But over all, few deny that Cabrini has been a safer, more liveable place.

In 1982, a year later, *The New York Times* announced that "Fear Returns to Project Where a Mayor Stayed." Not to be outdone, the *Chicago Sun-Times* in 1983 published the results of an intensive investigation entitled, "2 Years After Byrne's Stay, Cabrini-Green a Slum Again." The analysis concluded: "Now the pied piper is gone. But the rats remain, and life is back to normal at Cabrini-Green."

The CHA As Landlord

Gustav Master, a former executive director of the Chicago Housing Authority, defended the original idea behind federally financed public housing. Such housing was to be a way station for those temporarily unemployed or without income. Families that moved into public housing were not expected to remain poor very long; and the income limits would force them to move out so that others temporarily in poverty could take their place. Master was as emphatic as he was defensive:

> Make no mistake. The CHA is in the real estate business. We manage property. We rent apartments. We are *not* a social agency. We are *not* a social service organization.

As the city's largest landlord, Master had his hands full. He could be regarded as the "mayor" of 145,000 "official" CHA residents, making the CHA population larger than that of Peoria or Rockford. He managed 1,300 separate buildings, built at a cost of $635 million; monitored 45,000 rental leases; and supervised CHA's 2,300 workers. In vain, he tried to limit the CHA's responsibilities to brick and mortar, to building hardware. But he could not avoid the "software" side of a typical public housing project. While fewer than four per cent of Chicago's three million inhabitants live in family public housing projects, ten per cent of the city's homicides occur in public housing. Only four CHA projects are racially integrated with significant Hispanic or white tenancy; all four are low-rise projects, three stories or less. If the CHA population were to be ranked with that of the largest cities of the United States, only 110 cities would be larger.

Wendell Johnson, who managed Cabrini-Green for eleven of its best and worst years during the 1960s and early 1970s, concluded that:

> Cabrini-Green has become a "social hospital." But we don't have the supportive services that a good hospital needs. We don't have an intensive care unit for multi-problem households, for crippled families who need extraordinary loving care. We have become the

housing of last resort for young mothers with two or three children who don't know their fathers.

How do we help her or the kids? A first-class social hospital would help tenants get back on their feet, find a job, earn a decent income and swim back into the mainstream on their own.

Cabrini-Green doesn't have sufficient resources to help tenants overcome alcoholism, unemployability, drug addiction or juvenile delinquency. We have no way of barring doors to marauding males. How can we be expected to protect vulnerable girls? If ninety per cent of the families moving in are headed by unwed mothers with small children, the project's social environment discourages improvement.

Compared to the large donations which private givers make to Chicago's best hospitals, the amount spent in Cabrini-Green on rehabilitation and social support is a widow's mite. Living in Cabrini-Green should help residents move up the ladder. And we should be able to help them find that ladder.

Johnson, however, was not ready to be negative about Cabrini-Green as a whole:

One of my concerns about Cabrini-Green is the general reputation it has as a center of crime. It is certainly nothing of the kind. Yes, we do have crime problems. . . .But the vast majority of residents are decent, forthright individuals whose goals in life are just the same as you'll find among people living in the outer city and suburban areas.

The Management of Social Poverty

The reality of the hard-core poverty entrenched in the high rises has superseded the "up and out" philosophy that family public housing was to be a temporary residence. The wife of a retired minister who had served in Cabrini-Green voiced her own view of Cabrini-Green as a social hospital:

The project is the most sexist institution in Chicago. The females are highly visible. You could easily be persuaded that Cabrini-Green is inhabited only by grandmothers, sisters, daughters, aunts, nieces, godmothers, sisters-in-law and mothers. But where are the males? You'll find them girl-watching from corridors, lurking in hallways, loitering around saloons, scooting in and out of apartments. They're the project scavengers and predators. They take plenty but give little in return.

The man who takes his children to the park or church will do so on Sunday because he knows that the social worker will not be around that day. Finding him in the mother's apartment would jeopardize her monthly check from the Illinois Department of Public Aid.

The retired minister himself was not so comfortable characterizing Cabrini-Green as a social hospital:

> I prefer calling the project the Indian reservation of the 20th century. We allow the poor-poor to congregate here. Then we turn our backs on them. The project is confining, entrapping. You don't have to live there, but you do. You're riding the welfare merry-go-round. Someone else pays for your rent, food, or clothes and takes care of the medical bills. The schools are right on the premises or across the street. So are the churches. It's no sweat to stay. It's the leaving that is rough.

> I'm not surprised when a thirteen-year-old girl is asked, "What do you want to be when you grow up?" and quick as a flash she replies, "a public aid recipient." The young mothers not only watch out for their preschoolers but also for their monthly "salary check." That's what they insist on calling the welfare check.

Qualifying for public aid becomes, for many young and unwed mothers, the poor person's equivalent of a credit card or charge account. Success in entering the welfare system is a rite of passage that confers higher status on the teen-age mother. With her baby, she is no longer a cipher; she has become a somebody. She has her own case file, her own apartment (if she does not give up the child) and her own social worker. In her fight for a sense of worth and against a feeling of uselessness, her dignity is enhanced by the baby. She has now become the victim of a mischievous welfare system.

Managing Chaos

Is Cabrini-Green out of control? Have chaos and disorder been so institutionalized in high-rise buildings that the project syndrome has taken over? A resident asks the important question: "Which is the greater danger? Being mugged by a streetwise thug or by the system?"

The most dangerous public transportation system in Chicago is the Cabrini-Green elevator. In the better neighborhoods of Chicago and in the middle class suburbs, security and safety are awesome worries for residents. Elaborate alarm systems, outdoor lighting, doors with double locks, iron folding gates, large dogs and private guards help reduce the fear of home invasion. Strangers on the public streets are easily identified. The elevators in high rises that house the middle class have security guards around the clock.

But in the Cabrini-Green high rise, security is a jest, a will-of-the-wisp. The elevators are unguarded, even if they are working. Anybody can use them. They are preferable to the open stairways and partially secluded hallways which invite drug users, muggers, prowlers, purse snatchers and rapists. The stairways are recruiting grounds for gangs.

The recurring elevator crises in the vertical boxes which some people call family housing is a sign of a deeper and chronic malfunctioning. Unattended elevators were not designed to withstand use by boisterous teen-agers, by preschoolers rushing to play out-of-doors, by students hurrying indoors to relieve themselves in a fifteenth floor toilet or by street bums who wander into the building to ogle young girls. The president of the tenant council in a nineteen-story high rise points to an unguarded entrance on the first floor and says:

> This hallway is a tavern, and the stairway is the bathroom. You don't need a key to enter. It's a public place.

Who is in charge of Cabrini-Green? The tenants certainly are not. The CHA wants tenants to believe that it is in control. But its management policy is one of benign neglect. Vacancies are more numerous than officially reported. Deferred maintenance, broken windows and building repairs are understated in public statements. City Hall is not in charge, nor is the Chicago Police Department even though it wishes it were. On the other hand, the gangs hope they can persuade the outside world that they run the project. The powerlessness of Cabrini-Green residents is reflected in the experience of a former pastor of a church on the Lower North Side:

> No church here is self-supporting. The ministers and priests have to beg somewhere else for dollars to keep their doors open and their boiler heating.

> My congregation had a few old-timers who lived in Cabrini-Green; the rest were always newcomers. Seldom did they stay long enough to develop a loyalty to the church. Their financial generosity was not enough to pay the utility bills. I had to beg elsewhere to pay off the annual deficit.

External Forces

The truth of the matter is that living conditions, at Cabrini-Green and at other public housing projects with hundreds of vacancies, are usually beyond the control of residents. Their fate also lies in the hands of outsiders, the government bureaucracies whose chief interest is not the welfare of public housing tenants. Many of Cabrini-Green's ups and downs can be traced to outsiders ready to exploit Cabrini-Green for their own political gain. Examples of such exploitation are easy to pinpoint.

● Periodically, the empty apartments at Cabrini-Green provide ready-made places to house "early release" prisoners, evacuated from overcrowded state penal institutions. A Cabrini-Green social worker described what happened in 1981, two months before Mayor Byrne moved in:

> Suddenly, our sidewalks were taken over by adult males, all strangers. Where did they come from? Who were they? Nobody seemed to know, but we soon found out. They were "parolees," recent arrivals from the state prison, except that their parole officer didn't seem to know where they were. One of the new residents was officially recorded living at 160 North LaSalle Street, the State of Illinois office building downtown. He was here in Cabrini without the knowledge of his parole officer but with the cooperation of CHA staff who wanted the monthly rents.
>
> Nobody was surprised when we had an upsurge of gang activity.

A heavy concentration of ex-prisoners and former gang leaders, under little or no supervision, is not likely to generate a wholesome environment for anyone, especially for teen-agers living in Cabrini-Green.

● Cabrini-Green tenants are vulnerable to political exploitation. Some public figures will hitchhike on the project's notoriety to gain wider exposure for themselves in the media. That is one of the reasons why the Reverend Jesse L. Jackson appeared in Cabrini-Green in 1970 immediately after the two policemen on duty had been gunned down by a sniper's rifle. After a shower of television and newspaper publicity, he went elsewhere. A Cabrini-Green tenant commented on Jackson's quick entry and exit:

> Jackson is a celebrity. He knows it. So do we, as we welcomed the attention he got for us. He talked about us as the "soul coast" and them as the "Gold Coast." After finishing with us and getting national publicity, he left. I haven't seen him since.

A decade later in 1981, newspaper headlines reported eleven murders and thirty-seven persons wounded in Cabrini-Green during the first three months of that year. Shortly thereafter, Mayor Jane Byrne announced that she would move in. She spent three weeks there, off and on. During her stay, with heavy police escort, living conditions improved. Crime almost disappeared. Her stated reason for living in the apartment was:

> I refuse to give up another generation of our children to the gangs. . . .I'd like someone to tell me why the majority of problems at Cabrini. . .are gang-related and they [the gang leaders] are all parolees released early.

During the next two summers her husband, Jay McMullen, coached Little League baseball in a Cabrini-Green playground and came to know dozens of the youngsters. When the Mayor lost her bid for re-election in 1983, Cabrini-Green became easy to disregard. The *Chicago Tribune* quoted McMullen's explanation for his and her neglect:

> I recently ran into one of my pitchers, who asked: "Hey, Mr. Jay, are you gonna be running the team?" I said, "No, Lefty. We got beat, ya know."

Politics and Power

The political loyalties of public housing residents lie with the local Democratic Party, yet the tenants receive little in return. Is the situation similar to the Indians who, in 1626, gave the island of Manhattan to the Amsterdam Dutch in exchange for a few trinkets? A precinct worker from the influential 42nd Ward Democratic political organization disagrees. He says:

> The voters in my Cabrini-Green precinct have no clout because they can't sustain their political power. Everytime a leader appears, to demand a fair share of city services, that guy is six months away from moving out. If a woman shows enough spunk to complain, it's a sure bet that she possesses the drive to move elsewhere. And she does. Only the defeated or those personally involved in Cabrini-Green stick around.

> Do I live in my precinct? No. The voters who come and go make it easy for me to be an absentee political worker. I'm the only one around with enough experience to bring out the vote on election day.

Public housing projects are valuable political properties which the Democratic Party has a vested interest in preserving. A large public housing project is usually the ward's Democratic stronghold, housing "bread and butter" voters. On election day the tenants turn out overwhelming majorities for the Democratic ticket. Typically, they are not anti-establishment; they are accustomed to cajoling or manipulating the political system skillfully enough to get as many favors as they can.

In Cabrini-Green the 42nd Ward Democratic Party is the only organization that is omnipresent. Though neither highly visible nor especially vigorous, it does find jobs and take care of some personal needs, for example, tracking down a missing public aid check or providing free legal services to those who cannot afford them. But it feels incapable of dealing with the larger institutionalized problems, such as gang terrorism, frequent homicides, young teen pregnancies and elevator disasters.

Who then is in charge? Nobody, really. Cabrini-Green, like other high-rise projects in Chicago, is an administrative nightmare. Managers come and go. New management systems are tried. Operations are decentralized; new leadership is installed; city services are improved for a time; more professionals are employed; more training is given to existing staff. Some of these steps ease the pain and hardship that beset Cabrini-Green residents. But such changes have little impact on the project's social poverty. For the causes of the persistent poverty remain untouched. Each year dozens of Cabrini-Green apartments are removed from the rental market because of vandalism and wanton destruction. Cabrini-Green's three nineteen-story buildings, among the tallest of any high rises located in Chicago's public housing projects, are nicknamed "gun towers" by the residents. Homicide, robbery or rape is a weekly event. Each year the average age of mothers with their first child becomes lower. What happens to the psyche of a child who falls asleep to the nightly sounds of gunfire and of bottles crashing on the pavement below?

Is this an urbanized jungle? A place where human life is nothing more than a lion's kill? No. Behind the screaming headlines, there are the people of Cabrini-Green, struggling to survive — loving, hating, caring, searching, mourning — just as people do everywhere. But here along this branch of the Chicago River, as along the banks of the Upper Amazon, the fight for existence often ends brutally and abruptly.

The social and economic misery entrenched in Cabrini-Green is in its third decade. During this time, public and private programs to end the poverty have been singularly unsuccessful. Such efforts failed because the social poverty now lodged in Cabrini-Green is radically different than that of its predecessors in Kilgubbin and Little Italy. Chicago is confronted by a new urban poverty whose origins are not fully understood and for which remedies have yet to be found.

7

Public Housing's New Poverty

*The worst, the most corrupting
of lies are problems poorly
stated.* —Georges Bernanos

When Chicago's public housing was first constructed during the 1930s, it served a triple purpose: to clear the city's slums, generate jobs for unemployed building workers and house the working poor. It was viewed as interim shelter for families who would eventually leave to find decent housing in the private market. Devereux Bowly, Jr., noted that in the Ida B. Wells Homes, one of the first low-rise projects:

> An early endeavor of the tenants. . .was a "Get off and keep off the WPA and Relief" club. This group gathered job vacancy listings and made them available to project residents.

In those first years of public housing, broken families did not qualify. Only a "complete family," two parents with children, would be admitted. Furthermore, priority went to families who were living in substandard housing and whose income was inadequate to rent a good apartment in privately owned housing. *And all the buildings were low-rise.*

In 1950 the radical and destructive changes began. The first elevator buildings, six and nine stories high, were built. They revealed the Chicago Housing Authority's new love affair with high-rise living for families with children. The federal government supplied the money. With their superblocks of high-rise public housing, the new "vertical neighborhoods" would, to quote Elizabeth Wood, then the executive director of the Chicago Housing Authority, "compete with the suburbs for social desirability, especially for families with children."

Decades later the high-rise buildings, some twenty-two stories high, are still here — in varying stages of deterioration; some beg for major repairs. The occupancy also has altered drastically. Today, ninety per cent of the households with children are headed by women. Most rely upon public assistance. Past efforts to achieve racial integration either failed or were abruptly abandoned. Most of Chicago's public housing families are black.

Public housing was originally designed and built for the traditional poor, those whose breadwinner was out of a job or who was temporarily in financial trouble. It was not planned to hold and help the "new poor" who are predominantly the current residents of public housing.

In Chicago and elsewhere, public housing is in turmoil because of a massive shift in the character of urban poverty and in the nation's understanding of who is to be counted as poor. In the 1980s public housing managers have not succeeded in harboring the "new poor" in high rises without multiplying their numbers from one generation to the next. Why? The answer lies in the nation's failure to appreciate the elusive and changing character of this poverty and thus its causes and treatment.

The Changing Meaning of Poverty

After the Great Depression of the 1930s, the United States exhibited unbridled optimism about its ability to abolish poverty as it witnessed a dramatic decline in the number of poor. Poor people who were formerly the charges of social workers and religious reformers passed into the hands of economists. And soon poverty came to be defined predominantly in economic terms. An "official poverty level" was quantified and stated in dollars. Those who fell below that level were, by that very fact, "in poverty." "The official definition of poverty," according to the Congressional Budget Office, "classifies as poor those families whose money incomes are less than specified poverty thresholds that vary with family size and consumer prices," $10,650 for a family of four in 1985, for example.

This post-depression, income-based approach to poverty gave

fresh encouragement to social scientists who advocate that a society's "bottom fifth" in income always be regarded as poor. Their aim is to reduce the dollar gap between those in the top and bottom fifths of the population. The social scientists confuse, of course, inequality with poverty. While the two notions are related, they are not the same. If the lowest twenty per cent of the population is by definition poor, these people will indeed be around for as long as human life persists.

The quicksilver character of poverty is widely recognized. The emphasis during the Great Depression on poverty as primarily an economic condition did not surprise Herman P. Miller, former head of the statistical division of the U.S. Bureau of the Census. After examining the origins of poverty, Miller concluded:

> The word poverty, which is used so loosely, is in reality a very complex concept that can be defined, measured, and analyzed in many different ways. Like a chameleon, it takes on the coloration of the milieu in which it is used. It has one meaning in India and another in the United States. The meaning of poverty in America today is quite different from its meaning at the turn of the century.

In every age, each society defines poverty in its own way. Not so many years ago U.S. families were ineligible for public aid if they owned a television set, a telephone or a second-hand auto.

Optimism About Ending Poverty

A scion of the age of rising expectations, Herbert Hoover was the first to make the abolition of poverty a national political goal. In accepting the Republican nomination for the presidency in 1928, Hoover proclaimed:

> We in America today are nearer to the final triumph over poverty than ever before in the history of the land. The poorhouse is vanishing from among us. We have not yet reached that goal, but given a chance to go forward with the policies of the last eight years, we shall soon with the help of God be within sight of that day when poverty will be banished from this nation.

Hoover's prediction proved to be wrong. The stock market crashed on October 29, 1929. Economic depression followed, and millions of unemployed shamed the nation.

New Deal reformers of the 1930s used the depression experience to pass laws which viewed poverty primarily as insufficient income.

They focused on the social injustice of low wages, uncertain employment, depleted savings, credit unavailability, chronic joblessness and insufficient family income. To achieve social justice, income-producing measures had to be accorded first priority. Unemployment compensation laws, a farm credit administration, a legal minimum wage, social security and other income maintenance laws were enacted to redistribute income and thus ward off poverty.

Nearly forty years after Hoover had promised the abolition of poverty, two internationally renowned Democrats, also caught up in the revolution of rising expectations, made the same prediction and shared his euphoria. They were Wilbur J. Cohen, U.S. Secretary of Health, Education and Welfare, and Sargent Shriver, first director of the Peace Corps and the Office of Economic Opportunity, the federal agency which spearheaded the "war against poverty" in the 1960s. Keynoting a symposium at Georgetown University in 1968, Cohen hoped that the United States stood on the threshold of the last decade of poverty as a national problem. "I believe," he said, "that we can eliminate poverty in the Seventies." Appearing before a Congressional committee in 1967, Shriver testified:

No other legislature in the history of the world has urged the mobilization of the resources of a nation toward the total elimination of poverty.
— Rome gave the poor bread and circuses.
— The ancient Greeks threw their surplus grain to the poor.
— William the Conquerer provided land for the serfs.
— The Knights Templar invented the flophouse.
— The followers of St. Francis started the bread line.
— Nineteenth century England developed the dole.

But the Congress of twentieth century America had the courage and the vision to demand that poverty itself be ended. . . .

We may be divided on strategies for civil rights. We may be fragmented on issues of war and peace. We may be isolated by the generation gap. But we are a nation united on the eradication of poverty.

In their zeal to end poverty, Hoover, Cohen and Shriver reflected the Judaeo-Christian concern for the outcast, the misfit, the refugee and the poor. They spoke in the Talmudic tradition: "If all of the afflictions of the world were assembled on one side of the scale and poverty on the other, poverty would outweigh them all." They were conscious of the new possibilities inherent in the technological revolution of the 20th century. Historically, women and men had lived in societies of scarcity. In the western world of the 19th century the masses were still poor. In this century, however, social classes divided by poverty and wealth are cushioned by a large middle class.

Shriver and Cohen could find historical support on the North American continent for their optimism about poverty's early demise. Reporting in 1890 on slum poverty in New York City, Jacob Riis assumed that fifty per cent of the residents were poor when he wrote his urban classic, *How the Other Half Lives.* In 1937, less than a half century later, President Franklin Roosevelt saw "one-third of a nation ill-housed, ill-clad, ill-nourished." When Michael Harrington published *The Other America* in 1962, his great book of social protest, the proportion had dropped to one-fourth. Two years later, when President Lyndon Johnson declared "unconditional war on poverty," he targeted the "forgotten fifth" of the nation "who have not shared in the abundance." Poverty continued to decline steeply. By 1973 the U.S. Bureau of the Census could announce that the poverty rate had fallen once more — to one-ninth or eleven per cent — the lowest ever recorded in the history of the United States.

During these decades, those moving out of the ranks of poverty were the upwardly mobile poor, those for whom public housing was originally constructed — to tide them over throughout a time of financial stress.

The Unexpected Surge in Poverty

Despite favorable economic trends and the good intentions of federal officials, the downward trend in U.S. poverty was to be reversed: by 1982 the number in poverty had risen to one-seventh or fifteen per cent. A report from the Congressional Research Service of the Library of Congress found that "the share of people in poverty in the United States began a sharp rise in 1978 which continued through 1982 and now equals fifteen per cent of the population — the highest level since 1965." The report singled out "the progress against poverty in the 1959-1969 period, the plateau from 1970 to 1978, and the ground lost from 1979 to 1982." The trend is dishearteningly non-partisan: the U.S. poverty rate began to climb during the Democratic administration of President Jimmy Carter and continued doing so in the Republican era of President Ronald Reagan.

Every indicator since 1982 continues to forecast a steady rise in poverty. After a half century of bold initiatives to uproot poverty, mayors and public housing managers drown in statistics, puzzling over the growing poverty and demanding better explanations for its upsurge. The earlier optimism recedes in the face of rising poverty which is forcing a reexamination of the prevailing opinion that poverty represents only a shortage of cash income.

The crucial step in solving any problem is to define it as precisely as possible. Today's social poverty is a new urban phenomenon, more intractable than the transient poverty of the 1930s. It is this new social poverty, lodged in public housing among other places, that accounts for the millions of "new poor." Without discarding the federal government's dollar index of poverty, the search is underway for a holistic approach that would reduce the new poverty experienced today, thus deterring further explosions of the nation's latest social misery. Such an approach relies heavily on a non-economic definition of poverty. For the new social poverty defies explanation if the traditional notions of case poverty and mainstream poverty are used.

Mainstream Poor and Case Poverty

Those in *mainstream poverty* are the temporary poor. They are the ones most readily discerned by an income-based index. They are the families whose breadwinner has been laid off from work; households overwhelmed, for a time, by the staggering costs of illness or an accident; or homes visited by tragedy, for example, divorce, the death of a working parent, or migration caused by religious or political persecution. They include the low-income households for whom the federal government originally financed public housing — those temporarily in need of decent shelter. Much of the New Deal legislation and many of the Great Society programs targeted these transitional poor, most of whom would eventually escape the purgatory of joblessness. As prosperity increases, the number of mainstream poor decreases. During a recession or depression, their number multiplies. In summary, the mainstream poor are basically upwardly mobile, but detoured for awhile. With or without special programs to help them, these unemployed will eventually find jobs; and the working poor will gain higher incomes. The mainstream poor are usually not the households who now live in public housing projects like Cabrini-Green.

Prior to the depression of the 1930s, the notion of *case poverty* took precedence in the public conscience. Persons in case poverty suffered from some individual affliction: a chronic illness, mental handicap, physical disability, orphanhood. Case poverty, which dominated the social welfare perspective of the 19th and early 20th centuries, is not a modern invention; it rests upon a time-honored tradition.

Case poverty, therefore, designates the more or less permanent poor. They are the special cases: the physically disabled, the hard-to-place children, the drug addicts, the down-and-out alcoholics, the blind, the senile, the bed-ridden and the chronically ill. Unless they come from a family of means or marry into one, they have little hope of ever being self-supporting, although their descendants do. They usually do not enjoy the family resources which would make a difference in their lives. They are the poor found in sheltered workshops, houses of hospitality, halfway houses, sheltered care facilities, nursing homes, state institutions, special education classes and community mental health clinics. Mother Teresa of Calcutta knows a great deal about this kind of poverty.

For those burdened by case poverty, income redistribution schemes or full employment strategies seldom succeed. It is generally recognized that the ordinary escalators to lift them out of poverty are usually beyond their reach. "Except as it may be insufficient in its generosity, the society is not at fault. . .," John Kenneth Galbraith argues in *The Affluent Society.* He goes on to write:

> The most certain thing about this poverty is that it is not remedied by a general advance in income. Case poverty is not remedied because the specific individual inadequacy precludes employment and participation in the general advance.

In summary, case poverty includes those with an inherited or acquired handicap that limits their mobility, cuts off their easy access to the larger society or makes it difficult for them to cope with the discipline imposed by the modern world of work. Cabrini-Green provides shelter to hundreds who suffer from case poverty.

The New Social Poverty in Cabrini-Green

During the last two decades, as the quality of life in Cabrini-Green has worsened, it has been *social poverty* which has swelled the ranks of the poor. In contrast to the income-defined poor, social poverty describes overwhelming social disorder. Its social disorganization entwines the lives of those in similar straits, whereas case poverty is individualized.

Social poverty is a new urban condition, fundamentally different from anything previously known in the United States. The growing millions in social poverty include families abandoned by their fathers; the exploding population of teen-aged, unwed mothers who may be employable but not placeable; two-time offenders; adults who have never been employed and who are difficult to socialize; aging juveniles who are school dropouts, functionally illiterate, in contact with the courts and hard to employ; undocumented aliens; and street criminals. These are, as the Ford Foundation says, the "severely disadvantaged" who belong to the so-called underclass. In 1976 Mitchell Sviridoff, then vice-president for national affairs at the Ford Foundation, contended that the underclass

> is a sector of the poor who, for reasons we do not adequately comprehend, do not respond to traditional social service or income strategies — no matter how intensive the services and no matter how adequate the income. . . .

> Because we, as a society, have failed to make this critical distinction between the "underclass" and the poor generally, we have given credence to the increasingly fashionable notion that affirmative social policies do not work and may indeed be counterproductive. A careful examination of all the evidence leads me to a less simplistic conclusion: Many, though not all, social programs have been effective in helping very large numbers of the poor and minorities move out of poverty. At the same time these same programs have failed miserably with the underclass. . . . and overlook the more fundamental need for the development of new strategies and the refinement of existing ones to deal with this persistent and tangled web of pathology. . . .

In the United States, the new social poverty is the social equivalent of Karl Marx' lumpenproletariat of industrialized Europe.

The web of pathology, in which these poor are caught and from which escape is painful, snares victim and victimizer alike. It is a web of needless violence, gang extortion, the quick fix, helplessness, prostitution and rip-off. The hard-core poor are not in the urban mainstream nor are they the special "cases" of poverty. In mainstream poverty, generally speaking, a little private or public assistance goes a long way; in case poverty, where family resources are puny, outside aid becomes crucial. On the other hand, it is not clear what aid would stir those mired in social poverty to climb out.

Those in social poverty are natives, as New York Mayor Robert Wagner once pointed out, to "the underworld of poverty, today's invisible poor." Decades ago they were the rural poor to be found in the roadless hollows of Appalachia, in the Deep South, on Indian reservations or along the California and Texas trails migrant families followed. Nowadays, they populate urban areas, living in giant high-rise public housing projects like Cabrini-Green, in Newark's poverty-saturated areas or in Washington's misery-ridden blocks where the illegitimacy rate exceeds seventy per cent. To make things worse, the urban areas inundated by deep social poverty then become the reception centers for the helpless patients evicted en masse from state mental institutions. The social misery already in such areas is aggravated by high concentrations of sheltered care facilities, rehabilitation institutions and detoxification centers for alcoholics.

The increasing poverty among black households in any northern city is home-grown. It is to be found chiefly among blacks born and raised there and not among newcomers from the South. How is the intergenerational perpetuation of social poverty to be explained? In 1981 Martin Kilson, professor of government at Harvard University, wrote in *The Public Interest* that poverty

> is, on one level, rooted in the enormous expansion of female-headed households during the last two decades — a development first brought dramatically to public attention by Daniel Patrick Moynihan in a much-criticized but extremely useful study for the Department of Labor, *The Negro Family: The Case for National Action* (Washington, D.C., 1965). . . .

> What is unique about female-headed families is that all of them, regardless of race, display a seemingly endemic incapacity to foster social mobility comparable to husband-wife and male-headed families.

The concerned pastor of a church which ministers to Cabrini-Green residents characterizes this public housing culture:

> Pregnancy is a tremendous problem; it is the single largest occupation in Cabrini. These days most young girls do not have to drop out of school to have their children. A daughter's mother will take care of the child while the daughter goes back to school. It is an accepted thing in Cabrini-Green. A mother wants to

protect her daughter. To reduce the pregnancy and dropout rate among girls, the girls have to know that raising babies is not their only talent. There is also work and school.

Cabrini sons do not get the same message. Like everywhere else there is a double standard.

Grandmothers in their early thirties and children having children perpetuate social poverty into the next generation.

Reacting to the New Social Poverty

The appalling statistics about black social poverty and the precarious state of the black family spurred the nation's black leaders to unprecedented action. Eleanor Holmes Norton, former head of the U.S. Equal Employment Opportunity Commission, affirmed that the "strong growth in female-headed households is the central problem in black families and why poverty is so lasting." Father George Clements, pastor of Holy Angels Church in Chicago and one of the nation's black leaders, summed up his view of the situation:

> Black people have survived institutional slavery, economic injustice, wretched housing, staggering unemployment, inferior education, tragic crime and paralyzing poverty. Black people have survived every social ill America has ever known. . . .
>
> Now, lo and behold, a relatively new enemy rears its ugly head. This latest arrival contains far more potential for destruction than all of its predecessors combined. The most formidable enemy facing the black community today is the decay of black family life. The decay is far different from bad housing or rising unemployment. . . .The decay of the black family life comes from within — not from without.

Paradoxically, social poverty, among whites or blacks, is not yet a fixed and closed social class which entraps its victims into the second and third generation. Many youngsters and some adults do in fact find the vehicles for their mobility via, for example, excellent teachers, gainful employment or a church institution that has not deserted the poor. The alarming characteristic of the new underclass, however, is that those who remain behind grow each year in number. The mounting residue of social poverty, from year to year, guarantees that it will not, in the near future, disappear by itself.

A public consensus already exists about the best ways to reduce mainstream poverty and alleviate case poverty. No such consensus exists about social poverty. What is clear, however, is that traditional remedies have failed to reduce social poverty. The usual routines of treatment have simply not been very effective.

No other question among the nation's domestic issues looms so important. Why is social poverty so immune to the anti-poverty approaches so successful in the past? The answer is that the nature of urban poverty has changed. That is why old strategies are no longer as effective. New ones will have to be found.

Any mission to the poor living in public housing will have to rely, at minimum, on three basic strategies. The three deal not with the brick-and-mortar future of Cabrini-Green high rises but with their social environment, with the social conditions that restrain tenant opportunity. In part, these strategies are already being implemented, in and around Cabrini-Green, and they are described in the chapters that follow. In urban areas honeycombed with deep social poverty, ways have to be found to: *strengthen and revitalize* religious institutions, grass-roots groups, public and private schools and community-based services; *reduce* the isolation and alienation of families from the larger society of which they are a part; and *decrease* the pervasive dependency of families upon the governmental welfare system. By no means is this a complete list; it is a beginning.

Strengthening the Neighborhood Support System

Those in social poverty do not enjoy a neighborhood with sturdy social institutions, self-help organizations and community-based services to fall back upon in a time of crisis or minor emergency. Many of the churches, savings associations, fraternal societies, credit unions and settlement houses which once provided the newcomer with bridges into the urban society have fled Cabrini-Green and other public housing projects. Those institutions which remain fight for survival, beset by meager staffing, skimpy budgets, dilapidated equipment and outdated facilities. Ironically, the inner city parish struggles to pay an overdue energy bill, while the pastor of a wealthy suburban church splurges on air conditioning.

Educators, for example, complain that it is difficult to organize an active PTA in a poverty-dense school district. They are right. But it is also true that a strong PTA depends upon the continuity of school professionals who have the time to become friends of parents and who can deal, on a first-name basis, with students and community residents. If professionals are more transient than the residents they serve, what then? Migratory school principals and hosts of substitute teachers weaken the school as a neighborhood institution and inevitably undermine the impact of classroom education. The supportive social environment which is the lifeblood of a vital neighborhood relies upon the stable presence of pastors, youth workers, public health nurses, social service professionals and police officers. On the other hand, a high turnover rate and weak social institutions undermine the support that struggling, broken families desperately need to break out of the grinding cycle of poverty. Who is available, for example, to adopt the babies of unmarried black teen-agers in Cabrini-Green? In an emergency, where are the homes that will give youngsters loving foster care? At a "black family summit" in 1984, Dr. Robert B. Hill of the Bureau of Social Science Research in Washington, D.C., stressed the importance of traditional religious institutions.

> What did we do [before a Department of Health, Education and Welfare was formed]? We must return to a lot of basic institutions, like our churches that have always been significant resources.

That is why Father Clements continues to operate Holy Angels School, the largest black Catholic elementary school in the United States. A great many of its 1,350 students come from the public housing projects located in his parish. The tuition is $420 a year, plus fees and a parent's commitment to do fund raising. Planning is underway to construct a new school building at a cost of $7 million. To set an example for religious institutions, he adopted three teen-age boys and started a nation-wide crusade to encourage local church leaders to persuade black families to adopt homeless black children. He estimates that nationwide there are more than 100,000 such children. These are the youngsters facing the prospect of becoming adults in social poverty.

Reducing Alienation

It is no secret that social poverty isolates its victims from the rest of society. Where are the bridges to the outside world for tenants in a giant public housing project like Cabrini-Green? Where are the role models to stir the imagination and hopes of youngsters? Where is their job grapevine that passes on early news about job openings? Where are the families whose parents are cherished and whose children receive guidance, motivation and affection? The Catholic elementary schools which once steered the inner city's immigrant poor into the urban mainstream are disappearing one by one in the 1980s — even as social poverty grows worse. In the 1950s, four Catholic elementary schools and one Catholic high school served the Lower North Side; in 1986 only one school was left. Churches, community organizations, tenants' councils, self-help groups and community-based social services provide such bridges, networks, connections or influence. So do the professionals associated with these neighborhood groups.

On the other hand, the isolation and alienation of the public housing poor is worsened by truant officers, housing managers, precinct captains, counsellors, police officers, firefighters and even at times ministers — who live outside the community. They are not at hand when an emergency arises in the evening or early morning, at night or on weekends. A former City worker whose job took him in and out of Cabrini-Green argued for the presence of a neighborhood network around the clock and seven days a week:

> You can send into the projects all the service agencies you want to deal with the problems there. But when the sun goes down and the place goes dark, all those people in the service agencies go home. And who can blame them? At night is when the real problems begin. The only people left circulating in the projects are the cops and the gangs — with the residents inside their apartments with their doors locked.

If a poverty-ravaged neighborhood is already "redlined" by insurance companies and deserted by bankers and realtors, it is also forsaken by doctors, pharmacists, tailors, bakers, dentists, lawyers and other professionals.

An alumnus of Cabrini-Green, now a public school teacher, reflects on his own experience and that of others:

> Cabrini-Green is not a totally closed society. If it were, I would still be there — or in jail. The exit doors that I once used must be kept open so that other teen-agers and young adults can depart. They won't flee that poverty, however, without escorts, escape hatches or lifeboats. Who will continue to provide them?

In the search for solutions to poverty, we can highlight stories of success or failure; we can single out those who made it out of poverty or those who failed to do so. Sociologists, however, tend to concentrate on finding out why some people stay poor instead of discovering why others left their poverty behind. In the case of social poverty especially, the overriding question is why did some of the poor become better off? What inspirited them? How did they escape? What were the steps they took? How were they able to overcome obstacles of isolation and alienation?

The deepest divisions in U.S. society lie not between the rich and the poor or between blacks and whites, but between those with hope and those who have given up. Social poverty intensifies the isolation of the poor from two-parent families where the breadwinners enjoy steady employment and may even own the house in which they and their children live.

Decreasing the Dependency upon Government

Those in social poverty are held back because of restricted access to private resources. In a destitute community residents rightfully demand and often obtain government support. In the life cycle of the blighted inner city, public agencies have become all-important and omnipresent. Such an inner city area can be defined as one in which the government sector advances to fill the vacuum created by the departure of the private sector, both for-profit and not-for-profit. A giant public housing project like Cabrini-Green, for example, not only concentrates single-parent households receiving public assistance but also spins a tranquilizing web of government dependency. The poorest of the urban poor become utterly dependent upon public housing, public aid, a public medical clinic, government-funded training programs, the state job service, the county hospital, etc. Their mobility is restrained by a scarcity of private options. To lift themselves out of social poverty, tenants require multiple passageways to the private sector. What are such escalators out of poverty? The opportunity for a mother to bear her child in a private hospital rather than a municipal one. Active membership in a network that leads to a job in private business. The possibility of enrolling children in a non-public school. The chance to escape the ghetto by moving into privately owned housing, in a new neighborhood without wall-to-wall poverty.

A dilapidated inner city neighborhood is peopled in the main by low-income households whose livelihood depends upon some form of public assistance. In a neighborhood choking with poverty, the governmental presence is overwhelming. Family income levels are usually low, the prospects for neighborhood revival unpromising.

The private sector is in full retreat. The revitalization of such a neighborhood in any large U.S. city is inevitably accompanied by a substantial rise in the average income of tenants and property owners. Why? When privately owned buildings are rehabilitated, housing rents and purchase prices soar; only apartment seekers with high enough incomes are attracted. In some cases the heads of low-income families can afford to remain in the neighborhood if they find better paying jobs. But it is next to impossible to name an urban neighborhood where poverty has settled in but whose housing conditions have been visibly upgraded and whose commercial strips and religious institutions have undergone revival. The biggest single enemy of neighborhood improvement is the urban poverty which breeds dependency, neglect and despair.

In assessing the effectiveness of any government-funded welfare program, four questions always arise. Does it increase dependency or self-reliance, while trying to decrease poverty? Does it narrow or extend the recipients' range of choices beyond government? Does it enervate or strengthen personal responsibility, for example, the concern of fathers for their children? Does it dissipate the tenants' isolation and alienation from the world beyond the public housing project? For those in social poverty, near-total reliance upon government has all the earmarks of the 19th century paternalism of the company-owned town and its company store. Nowhere in Chicago is this wardship more evident than in Cabrini-Green. The advice of Martin Luther King, Jr., is as relevant today as it was in the 1960s:

> We must not let the fact that we are victims of injustice lull us into abrogating responsibility for our own lives.

Not all who call Cabrini-Green home are there because of social or case poverty, even though their number multiplies. Despite the web of social dependency, scores of Cabrini-Green families are in temporary poverty. They move out and find housing in the urban mainstream, in privately owned dwellings. Having left Cabrini-Green, they become its alumni and alumnae. Their stories about the ways to climb out of poverty help illuminate, by contrast, the dehumanizing character of the new social poverty. Their experience underlines the importance of the three strategic approaches just described: strengthening the neighborhood support system, reducing alienation and decreasing the dependency upon government.

8

Cabrini-Green Alumni

Free will and determinism, I was told,
are like a game of cards. The hand that is
dealt you represents determinism. The
way you play your hand represents free
will.—Norman Cousins, *This I Believe*

In seeking to explain a low-income, inner city neighborhood, sociologists look for victims, the social casualities of abnormal behavior and desperate poverty. Experts in the post mortem, sociologists dissect failure. When they enter a slum or ghetto, what do they find? According to a public health nurse, who is escorted daily into Cabrini-Green, they

> find those who stayed behind. The victims who tried to leave but never made it. Those who have been defeated. And those who still struggle to escape.

Despite Thomas Carlyle's reference to economics as a "dismal science," modern-day economists are more likely to identify with the achievers, the successful, the upwardly mobile. Economists in the United States are direct descendants of Horatio Alger. They are predisposed to analyze success. Why did this family make it? How did these youth move up and into the system? Hence economists shy away from Cabrini-Green and gravitate to the Gold Coast.

Social workers and social reformers, however, gravitate to a public housing project. Here is where they feel at home. Cabrini-Green's disconcerting statistics about crime, grade school pregnancies, drugs and gang violence are undeniable. But they are not the entire story. According to the same public health nurse:

> You can highlight the losers. Or single out the winners. But if you want the whole story, include them all.

There is another side to Cabrini-Green, largely unknown and seldom recognized: the graduates of Cabrini-Green. Margaret Smith, the eternal optimist who worked at Lower North Center for five decades, insists that "success profiles" could be written about hundreds of black women and men who have passed through Cabrini-Green. She recalls, for example:

> Ramsey Lewis, Jr., the jazz pianist; Curtis Mayfield, singer and composer; Eric Monte, script writer for television and movies; Anthony J. Watson, a graduate of the U.S. Naval Academy with a high command post on an atomic-powered submarine; Keithen Carter, an artist whose work has been exhibited at the Art Institute of Chicago and in galleries coast to coast; Solomon Greer, a medical doctor; Benjamin Martin, who went to Northwestern University and became a lawyer; John D. Hayes, president of the Chicago Bar Association in 1984; Marion Stamps, executive director of the Chicago Housing Tenants Organization; and Gloria Leggett-Brown, business manager of WGN television news in Chicago.

The Norris Family: A Profile

That roster of names, Margaret Smith says, could easily be expanded into a Cabrini-Green *Who's Who*. It would also include Howard Norris, another Cabrini-Green alumnus who earned a degree of Master in Public Administration from the University of Pittsburgh in 1974. With his wife and two children, he now lives in a suburb south of Chicago and works for the U.S. Small Business Administration. Norris recalls his youth in the public housing project:

"Ma was from the Deep South, from Belzoni in rural Mississippi. She used welfare as an interim means to care for her children until she found steady work.

"For her, public aid — or a project apartment — was a temporary setback to be overcome. For us, her family, moving into a row house in Frances Cabrini Homes in the early 1950s was a step up. We left a four-room flat, with no central heating, no hot water, no bath. Six of us shared the four rooms. There were two bedrooms. At night, the kitchen became a third.

"In the project, we enjoyed central heat and hot water. Most important, I only had to share my room with my brother. Now I could take a private bath without being on display in the kitchen.

"After we settled in, my mother worked as a domestic, a housekeeper. By age ten, I rode with her on Saturdays out of Cabrini, to Evanston, Wilmette and other suburbs. These trips made a big impression on me as a kid. They changed my picture of the world outside. I remember the big green lawns, the large stone houses and their libraries. I discovered another world — educated and moneyed people who could afford to hire my mother. They owned property and often their own businesses. This experience helped me shape my life goals. When I learned that they worked for themselves, I was more than impressed. At twelve, I was intrigued and spellbound.

"By the time I was thirteen, I had made up my mind. I no longer wanted to live in the project. I realized how important education was to make that dream possible. By fifteen I knew that books were the key to my self-development. My mother cajoled and nagged. Abe Smith, my brother, inspired me, set a good example. My teachers were tough. The public schools were good.

"Between fifteen and eighteen, during high school, I acquired street smarts, book sense, and my mother's wits. Mother's wits meant common sense and knowing how to use it. While gangs were in the neighborhood, I ignored them. I liked girls but knew better than to get any pregnant. I spent summers in Nashville with my grandmother, aunt and uncle. They were loving and kind. My uncle taught me how to play checkers and lose with grace.

"I was touched by many adults, from different walks of life. They cared about me as a kid. To them, I was a person. Alma Morgan taught art at Wells High School. She was short. I was taller. She talked and acted six feet. And her hair was red. She was my freshman homeroom teacher. I'll always remember her words to my class in 1963:

> Don't lie to me. Come to school on time. Don't make excuses. Don't write notes for your parents. Don't cut class. If you do any of these things or break my rules, you will answer to me or your parents. See this ruler? I'll use it on your hands if need be. You want help? Just ask me.

Again and again, I recall her telephoning parents at home or visiting students where they lived. If we needed help with homework, she would be there in the homeroom or in the study hall. Other teachers pushed me too. Wells High School was unique in this regard. In those days public high school students from the Cabrini row houses went to Wells High.

"At thirteen I started my first job as a delivery boy at a neighborhood grocery. The store was owned by Phil who was a Jew and a short, butterball of a man, and Burt, a skinny, white Anglo-Saxon Protestant. Every summer, all through high school, I earned extra money to pay for books and clothes and to help my mother with expenses. By my senior year, I was an apprentice butcher.

"Phil and Burt were indeed exceptional human beings. They taught me that math was needed to price items correctly and to make a profit. They taught me that if you treated customers and suppliers with respect, you will get the same in return. I learned that each white merchant was an individual and that they could not be judged fairly by the usual stereotypes. I watched them cut meat, put up stock and produce, handle the cash register, do the inventory, hire personnel, and do the jobs needed to operate the store. They owned the store but were never afraid to do any of the jobs for which they had hired others to do. Those lessons from my teen-age years helped me a great deal when I went to work in another world far from Cabrini.

"Looking back, I realize that I grew up in a neighborhood. Our Cabrini row houses were a community. Everybody knew your name, your mother, father, sister or brother. Parents looked out after each other's kids. We had an extended family. There were no strangers. We had neighborhood businesses that gave us part-time jobs and taught us responsibility. The Chicago Housing Authority staff knew every family personally. They knew your parents by name. If something was wrong with the apartment, they would see that it was fixed. We had flowers, grass and fresh paint once a year. The CHA staff inspected the apartments regularly to ensure that housekeeping standards were high. These were the early years of Cabrini-Green. We lived in Frances Cabrini row houses during the years that the high rises were built and occupied.

"After 1958, our row-house neighborhood was slowly destroyed by the addition of the red and gray high rises. We felt overwhelmed and inundated by the family-crowded high rises. From our point of view, the project had become asphalt, concrete and brick — an urban jungle. The project itself had changed inside and outside. It had become a place which traps people, much like a prison but without bars.

"My life changed drastically too. I left Cabrini-Green to go to the University of Dubuque in Iowa on a scholarship and then to Fisk University in Nashville. I turned twenty. I married Barbara J. Gaffney, a Cabrini girl. We were childhood sweethearts. With her support, I finished college and then obtained a master's degree from the University of Pittsburgh. Later, my wife earned her own college degree in accounting from the Illinois Institute of Technology. She worked days and went to school at night. She was graduated with honors.

"You could say that we became 'upwardly mobile.' We have two children, Howard Dubois and Tanya Ester. We were renters at first. Ten years ago we bought our first home. After living on the south side of Chicago, we moved in 1983 to a new home in a southern suburb to send our children to a better public school system.

"When we left Cabrini we never came back. Given today's circumstances, we have no reason to return."

Howard Norris is one alumnus of Cabrini-Green. There are a thousand and one other stories about women and men who grew up in Cabrini-Green, left it and found a future elsewhere. Their life histories deserve the attention of the urban pessimist.

Who Remains?

Not all Cabrini-Green residents, however, cross the bridge that will take them to another world. Not all hail Cabrini-Green as their alma mater. At the end of 1982, according to the CHA, forty-nine per cent of the heads of households had lived there at least seven years. In the Cabrini row houses, the oldest section of the project, fifty-nine per cent were tenants in 1974 or earlier. How then does one characterize the mobility of Cabrini-Green households? Generally speaking, they fall into three groups: those who remain by their own choice; those anxious to depart like Howard Norris; and those who seem not to care one way or the other.

● Many residents prefer to stay in Cabrini-Green. Some are older people who have settled in, for the rest of their lives, with a circle of friends, neighbors and church contacts. Others are, for example, like the father of a large family, who understands the importance of rent tied to income. His rent is low. If he loses his job as a security guard, the rent drops to match his income. Where else could he find a four-bedroom apartment, utilities included, for $90 a month?

Mrs. Janie Frye, who lives in a seven-story building with her three teen-age children, explains why she is there:

> I'm not planning to go anywhere. I consider my apartment a low-income condo. If my neighbors took the same pride in the inside of their apartments as I do, it would look like Carl Sandburg [Village]. I think it's going to get better. I don't know how long it's going to take, but I'm going to stay here and find out.

Residents like Lillian Swope, president of the Cabrini-Green tenants' council, have not lost hope. They pin the badge of responsibility for terror and violence on a handful of tenants and on the CHA's indifference. She and other tenant leaders have dedicated themselves to revamping conditions in the project. That is why they remain. John Dexter, who has lived in Cabrini-Green for twenty years and who once headed its tenants' council, is another optimist. He explains why he stays:

> Our youngsters look to us for leadership, as gangs compete with us for loyalty and attention. We need confidence that things will get better.

Another resident committed to staying in Cabrini-Green echoed Dexter's view about resident leadership:

> Cabrini Green can be one of the best places in which to live if people are not afraid and will stick together; if people would stop backing their children when their children are in the wrong; if people would not stand by and see their loved ones killed or crippled. By getting up and making a move, the violence would stop.

One of the oldest residents in a Cabrini row house spoke with pride about her durability as a public housing tenant: "Living here is the closest thing I know to owning a home of my own. My row house has been my home for nearly forty years."

Who Leaves?

● A second group of residents is eager to leave Cabrini-Green. Who are they? A few were among the 4,000 Chicagoans, mostly mothers, who blocked State Street on a cold winter morning in 1984, jamming a downtown office building to apply for federally subsidized housing in *privately owned* dwellings. The Leadership Council for Metropolitan Open Communities was scheduled that morning to distribute 1,000 applications to interested CHA residents and to those on the CHA waiting list. To avoid the danger of someone being trampled or pushed through a plate glass window, the registration was postponed. Hundreds of people had been in line before dawn; some had arrived the night before to camp inside the building. The outpouring demonstrated not only the wide need for decent, moderately priced housing, but also the desperation of parents who wanted to avoid living in a public housing project.

Then there are families who send their teen-agers to live with relatives during the summer or who enroll their youngsters, at great personal sacrifice, in private schools. Joyce Johnson, for example, has a fixed date for moving out. The mother of three daughters (two of whom are twins), she sends them to Josephinum, a Catholic high school. Their combined tuition costs her more than $2,000. Inexpensive public housing enables her to pay for a good private education for her children. But she awaits the day when they can forsake Cabrini-Green:

> I want a way out, and I'm going to get out. But for now, I can't. If I move out, I couldn't afford to pay for their schooling. So I have to stay here in order to help them.

In 1949 Johnny and Virginia Watson moved into a Cabrini row house and began to raise their six children. He worked sporadically in a coin laundry around the corner, while she worked as a teacher's aide. At the time of his death thirty-three years later, he and his wife still lived at the same address. But their six children, now grown, had left. One daughter had become an auditor for the Federal Reserve Bank, another the wife of an Air Force serviceman in California, and the third an engineering student at Purdue University. One son had become an accountant, the second worked for the *Chicago Sun-Times,* while the third served as a commander aboard a U.S. Navy submarine.

Who Seems Not to Care?

● The first two groups of Cabrini-Green households have made their decisions. But the third group, drifting in a day-to-day existence, typifies the new urban social poverty. Who are they? They are mainly young mothers with small children, who typify the matriarchal character of Cabrini-Green society. They are the teen-age, unwed mothers victimized by footloose men. They are out of the mainstream, utterly dependent upon public housing, public assistance, public health nurses, government clinics and the county hospital. They have few contacts and fewer opportunities in the private sector, in the world outside of Cabrini-Green. They are resigned, often with abiding bitterness, to the welfare system. They feel helpless, powerless and deserted.

Lieutenant Robert Curry, who headed the Cabrini-Green police patrol in 1983, described a child in one such family:

> We had to track down an eleven-year-old with a gun. The youngster was hunting his victim whom he had been hired to kill. We finally located him. He was the most amoral kid I ever met. He didn't know that what he was doing was wrong. What had happened to him?
>
> Illinois law says that as a kid under twelve, he cannot commit a crime. We had to let him go. He was probably back in his living room, enjoying television, before we finished our paper work on him.

The women who head Cabrini-Green households look for security inside the high-rise walls, behind barred and battered doors. Their sense of helplessness is evident in the despairing reply of one resident who was asked if she and her family had sufficient police protection:

> What can they do? I guess they do their best, but when the sun goes down, they are as scared as we are.
>
> Night don't really turn into day here. It's always night.

Future Alumni

Cabrini-Green residents will continue to leave. Father Sebastian Lewis, O.S.B., pastor of St. Joseph Church which supports an elementary school located down the street from Cabrini-Green, points out:

> Turnover among our students is high. Why? Many come from families ready to leave Cabrini. Though half of our students come from Cabrini, their parents scrape and save to raise the $720 yearly tuition per family. Some of our graduates go on to private high schools.

The failure to report income is widespread in America; it is also present in the "tax free" underworld of Cabrini-Green. Often enough, that money is channeled into drugs and alcohol, sinking its users even deeper into poverty. On the other hand, that cash enables a parent to send a child away for the summer to live with a relative in another city or to pay the tuition in a private school, thereby graduating another generation of successful Cabrini-Green alumni.

While coming from another CHA project, Kimberley Reads is typical of Cabrini-Green youths, like Howard Norris, who see college as their passport out of public housing. A tennis player, she was awarded a tennis scholarship at the University of Alabama. Her ambition, however, is to enrich the lives of children:

> I want to be an athlete. I want to play a lot of tennis. But I don't want to be a tennis pro. I'd rather be a recreation teacher.

Her hero is Arthur R. Ashe, a former world tennis champion who grew up in a public housing project. He gave this advice to her high school audience:

> My message is always the same. For every hour you spend on the athletic field, spend two in the library. Even if you make it as a pro athlete, your career will be over by the time you are thirty-five.

Louis Hill, fourteen years old and an eighth grader at the Jenner Public School in Cabrini-Green, is not a tennis player. In 1984 he won the 15th annual Illinois Poet Laureate Award for this poem:

My World

My world is a place of beauty
where the word Joy
is celebrated for a holiday.

My world has a place
for all the poor to sleep,
and food for the hungry.

The flowers smile in the glowing sun
and people dance to the sound of music.

In my world
there is no such word as
Violence.

My world is the sweetest place to be.

Young Louis Hill did not remain long in Cabrini-Green. Shortly after his graduation, he and his mother moved out.

Cabrini-Green is a bittersweet place.

9

No Easy Choices

Ideas have consequences, bad ideas
have bad consequences. —Jeane J.
Kirkpatrick

By 1990 Chicago's political establishment will face its single most important planning decision: the disposition of the public housing projects which rim the central business district. These family-occupied projects, mostly high rises, stymie the urban revitalization now proceeding north, south and west from the central business district. Just north of Chicago's downtown sits Cabrini-Green. To the west are the Grace Abbott, Henry Horner and Jane Addams projects. And to the south there is the Raymond Hilliard project, the first in a four-mile corridor of high-rise projects, including Robert Taylor Homes, along South State Street.

Urban revitalization is about to collide with these projects. It is already doing so on Chicago's Near West Side where neighborhood revival already surrounds one public housing project, while inching toward another. At the University of Illinois campus nearby, a professor who lives in the area made this observation:

> The Jane Addams housing project is an island in an ocean of renewal. On all sides, the project is surrounded by government initiative and private enterprise. University of Illinois buildings. Hospital expansion. Rehabbed homes. Modern town houses. Successful businesses. Dormant churches coming alive.

On a Collision Course

Similarly on the Lower North Side, new construction and rehabilitation inch their way closer to Cabrini-Green. M.W. Newman, an urban affairs writer for the *Chicago Sun-Times,* noted:

> Cabrini-Green now stands in precisely the right place to impede
> the elite, multi-million dollar, Near North renewal rolling west-
> ward.

The federal and city governments have thus far managed to dodge
the confrontation. It was they who built and still support the public
housing towers that impede further community improvement in
older Chicago.

Furthermore, these high-rise concentrations of poverty lock low-
income households into Chicago and keep them out of the working
class suburbs several miles to the west. Were these giant public
housing projects not available, many tenants would have already
located there.

In Chicago, however, further urban gentrification is not only
inevitable but also necessary. It will occur slowly in the communities
close to the lakefront and in others bordering the central business
district. Without it, many more buildings would be abandoned, for
they need extensive repair and tender loving care. Speaking of such
neighborhood change, Richard Taub, a professor of social science
at the University of Chicago, says:

> I am not an enemy of gentrification. . . .If we compare the
> amount of housing lost to people by being gentrified. . .to the
> amount of housing lost by abandonment and the lack of repair
> and attention, it's like comparing apples and oranges. The
> amount of housing lost through abandonment far exceeds the
> number of houses being deconverted.

High-Rise Public Housing: The End of an Era

The intellectual and moral foundations necessary to shorten the
life of high-rise public housing have been in place for more than a
decade. Widespread agreement exists that local governments, in
collusion with federal officials, made a colossal error in the 1950s
and 1960s. Working together, these governments erected giant high
rises for low-income families with children.

For the CHA and other public housing authorities, those decades
were the golden era of "the super block," the newest *vertical*
neighborhood. These were decades of good intentions and
boundless euphoria about the value of planning for the city's future
— ignited by a generous supply of federal dollars. The optimism of
public housing planners, however, was soon replaced by over-

whelming disappointment. Karla K. Powell recalled the Chicago experience:

> Having a father who was instrumental in implementing public housing is something I would never mention, much less brag about, with all the Monday morning quarterbacks I had to contend with.
>
> Yet I knew his motives were noble, and I felt anguish over the result. One night in particular, as we drove past Cabrini-Green, he conveyed a painful reconciliation with reality that didn't jibe with their best-laid plans.

Lawrence Amstader, an architect who designed the nineteen-story Cabrini-Green buildings, also recalled that:

> At the time we thought we were God. We thought we were doing something wonderful. . . .Back in those days, public housing was considered charity. It wasn't your God-given right like social security. So it had to look economical, it had to give the impression of being inexpensive. For example, it actually cost more to have the painter paint the address numbers on the buildings than it would have to put up metal numerals. But I wasn't allowed to put up numbers because it looked expensive.

That multi-billion dollar building program, however well-intentioned, produced a man-made urban disaster, the worst of the 20th century. Into these high rises, public housing agencies packed families, many prone to delinquency, crime and dependency. Income ceilings forced out upwardly mobile families who might have served as models for less mobile ones. The high rises fostered a social environment in which residents had little chance to kick the habit of poverty. New racial ghettoes were founded, replacing older buildings occupied, in the main, by two-parent families.

The high-rise mania eventually subsided. The federal courts finally became disillusioned with family high rises. The era of hyperelation — that large public housing projects would eliminate city slums — ended in 1970. The CHA's revised policy addressed not only the height of public housing buildings but the size of projects as well. Family high rises were outlawed, but so were all large "projects." Large housing complexes, even low-rise ones, would no longer be built. The CHA gave public notice:

> No family housing was permitted to exceed three stories, and all units were to be of low density and constructed by private contractors on scattered sites throughout the city. . . .

'Where Do You Want It?'

The new public policy, demanded by a federal court, was firm: new high rises would serve only the elderly, not families.

By publicly confessing in 1970 that high-rise projects threatened the health and welfare of families and by banning their further construction, the CHA was caught in a dilemma. If such buildings were that dangerous, what would the CHA do with the 168 family high rises (twenty-three in Cabrini-Green alone) it had already built and was ineffectively trying to manage? The replacement cost for all 168 buildings would approach one billion dollars. Relocating their 19,700 families would be a monumental task. The CHA did commission studies to determine whether a family high rise might be successfully converted to exclusive use by the elderly. It also invited private social welfare agencies, day care centers, boys clubs, and youth centers to work inside the projects.

From Bad to Worse

The embarrassing fact, fifteen years later, is that these housing projects are still around. All 168 high-rise structures remain in place — only in greater disarray, still deteriorating, and many losing their population. The CHA itself provided stark testimony about the condition of its high-rise projects. A CHA-appointed Committee on Problem Families, composed of staff and tenants, issued a report in 1981. Although restrained in its rhetoric because of its quasi-official status, that report to the CHA board detailed how living conditions had retrogressed in the large housing projects:

> The increase in number of children born out of wedlock, instances of unauthorized occupancy, use of apartments as "hangouts," and reports of gambling, prostitution and drug traffic in apartments leased to young, single-parent families has had a deleterious effect on some of our housing developments.

> The increase in poor housekeeping among families. . .has exacerbated the infestation problem in some of our developments.

> The increase in the number of emotionally disturbed families and elderly has created fear and apprehension among residents at some housing developments. Moreover, some staff lack the training and experience to deal with this type of problem.

> The failure. . .to understand and appreciate the serious crime problems in public housing sometimes results in lenient sentences and the early release and return of criminals to our public housing developments.

The report of the Committee on Problem Families once more set off an alarm, warning City Hall to pay attention. The alarm was ignored again.

'The' CHA Waiting List

A further source of consternation about the future of high-rise projects for families arises from information provided by the CHA about its elusive and mysterious "waiting list." Officially, that list chronicles applications for family housing. The number of applications nearly doubled in three years, swelling from 13,323 families at the end of 1980 to 24,000 by the end of 1983. A former CHA employee who had tried unsuccessfully to understand the workings of the list explained why he gave up his pursuit:

> Answers differ about the waiting list's age. One claims it's ten years old. Another says it is five. Then I'm told it is updated every two years. Everybody knows that the list is ignored for income-eligible families made homeless by a fire or by an encroaching public improvement. Politicians and others with clout can bypass the list to place "their" family.

> I know that CHA uses the waiting list, but its most valuable purpose is to provide a statistic big enough to bolster the case for more federal dollars for public housing.

That waiting list haunts the CHA. On the one hand the CHA routinely reported at the end of 1983 that 24,000 hopefuls remained on the list. Yet, two months later, the CHA advertised in the daily *Chicago Defender* that there were vacancies in six of its largest projects including Cabrini-Green. That startling newspaper ad announced that vacant apartments, ranging in size from one to five bedrooms, were available. (See advertisement on next page.)

What had happened to the waiting list? Why wasn't it being used? What did the *Chicago Defender* ad really mean? What did it reveal about Cabrini-Green and the other five public housing projects?

More households on the CHA waiting list were refusing to move into these six projects. In Cabrini-Green's 3,600 apartments, for example, the overall vacancy rate was reported as eleven per cent, even after Mayor Jane Byrne had come and gone as a resident in 1983. Furthermore, in the eight high rises which comprise the "William Green" section of Cabrini-Green, the vacancy rate for its 1,100 apartments was more than twenty-nine per cent.

Advertisement in the *Chicago Defender*,
February 29, 1984

Without intending to do so, that advertisement made public the locations of CHA's six most troubled housing projects for families, those continually tormented by broken elevators, frequent homicides, gang extortion, boarded-up windows, illegal squatters, graffiti-spattered hallways and vandalized apartments unfit for human occupancy. The six projects are dominated by high-rise buildings, discredited by high vacancy rates, occupied predominantly by single-parent families, and scarred by the increasing number of apartments requiring major repairs. In all, the six projects contain 100 high-rise buildings, sixty per cent of the 168 high-rise towers owned and managed by the CHA. These troubled projects are the ones usually avoided by the great majority of applicants for CHA-owned housing. A member of the CHA staff who works downtown, where the waiting list is kept, illuminated the seeming contradiction between an enormous waiting list and the high vacancy rates in the six projects:

> When they come in to fill out an application for a CHA apartment, they specify the projects which they prefer and those which they don't want. The outlying low-rise developments are top choice, since they seem to be the best for raising a family. Few people apply for the more notorious high rises like those in Cabrini-Green. The applicants are not dumb. They know the score.

Sometime between now and the end of this century, City Hall will be compelled to devise a plan for the disposition of the Cabrini-Green high rises, especially those over seven stories. Ever since 1970 when the Chicago Housing Authority, prodded by the federal courts, ceased further construction of housing projects for families with children, the City has postponed making a decision about the high rises.

The urban revitalization slowly encircling Cabrini-Green, however, is forcing a choice. The procrastination, which enabled mayors in the past to duck a confrontation over Cabrini-Green's future, is being challenged, steadily and successfully. Three reasons undermine traditional rationalizations for doing nothing. They compel City Hall to face what was once politically untouchable: (1) the high rises have begun to self-destruct; (2) the federal government is reluctant to spend more tax dollars to preserve the high rises; and (3) a political compromise may be around the corner.

1. No Longer Defensible

First, several of the Cabrini-Green high rises are deteriorated and dangerous. Upkeep by the CHA is haphazard, insufficient and more responsive to a television story than to a legitimate tenant complaint. Entire floors are empty with windows boarded up. Squatters abound and live next door to rent-paying tenants with signed leases. The vandalism of walls, windows, hallways, cabinets, stoves, elevator equipment, heating and electrical fixtures, doors and plumbing is unending. Almost everywhere, walls are splattered with graffiti. There are innumerable violations of health, building and fire codes, such as combustible trash in hallways and in vacant apartments.

There is no indication that either the Chicago Housing Authority or the U.S. Department of Housing and Urban Development is eager to spend the estimated $800 million needed to rehabilitate 104 projects city-wide; to bring them up to the standards of the City's building code; and at the same time to make them attractive enough (including the landscaping and exteriors) so that reliable tenants will want to move in. It is highly unlikely that such conditions would ever be met because the CHA would have to make sure that other high rises do not self-destruct as it begins to spend hard-to-get dollars on rehabilitating the worst buildings. For these and other reasons, the public clamor for upgrading the high rises is subsiding; it is seen as an impractical, illusionary alternative.

The attitudes of CHA leaders are changing. In previous decades, CHA's officialdom was adamant: no high rise would ever be demolished. Charles Swibel, who headed the Chicago Housing Authority for two decades, vowed repeatedly: "We'll never tear down Cabrini-Green. Never." In recent years, however, a new generation of CHA officials is reluctant to make such an unconditional promise. The opinion of these CHA executives appears irrelevant. Without any official authorization, the family high rises head for self-annihilation. One at a time, they become uninhabitable and slowly begin to self-destruct from constant abuse, postponed upkeep, second-rate management and little or no money to finish essential repairs.

2. The Federal Outlook

Secondly, pressure on the CHA to do something about the high rises also comes from the federal government. The U.S. Congress grows increasingly reluctant to fund housing projects with social conditions like Cabrini-Green's. The executive branch of the federal establishment seeks less expensive and more humane ways to provide the poor with decent housing. Federal judges have already banned further U.S. subsidies to build high rises for families with small children. The federal judiciary, however, has yet to face the question of what to do with the high-rise public housing which would not have been built had the court been wise enough to take earlier action.

The extensive disillusionment with high-rise housing among all three branches of the federal government has not yet crystallized into public policy. Any local initiative to eliminate gradually high-rise public housing for families is likely to be viewed sympathetically by federal officials. One such official shrewdly observed:

> Congress is not willing to appropriate the billions of dollars which would be required to rehabilitate and modernize the public housing projects, from coast to coast, which are in trouble. The rising federal deficit generates a Washington climate hostile to such a gigantic expenditure. Furthermore, the housing experts in HUD, whether Republicans or Democrats, see such money going down the drain and producing no lasting improvement in the troubled projects.

As of 1986, the federal government had invested more than $1.5 billion in the public housing operated by the CHA.

3. A Workable Compromise

Finally, as the legal population of Cabrini-Green declines and as the number of residents in neighboring blocks increases, political power is being redistributed. The voting strength of new residents who settle in the vicinity of Cabrini-Green upsets the historic balance of power and will ultimately attract the attention of elected officials. No longer are privately owned buildings in the vicinity of Cabrini-Green being systematically destroyed. Instead they are being conserved, restored and occupied. On the Lower North Side's vacant tracts, more new housing is being built. The incoming owners and renters, regardless of their race, are upwardly mobile, urban pioneers. A local precinct worker underscored the political consequences of the demographic shift:

> With fewer adult residents in Cabrini-Green, the number of registered voters is declining rapidly. They have been faithful Demo-

crats. (The local oddball is a Republican.) But the empty precincts around Cabrini-Green have started to fill up. That's the important difference. As the ranks of new voters multiply, local politicians will turn up their hearing aids. They will have to listen to, and deal with, their new, highly articulate, well-educated constituents. The new voters will not be satisfied with evasive answers or the warmed-over platitudes about Cabrini-Green.

Candidates for the position of alderman, ward committeeman, Illinois representative, state senator and congressman will find themselves in the middle. Their newly registered voters will demand changes in the project. On the other hand, the traditional voters living in Cabrini-Green will be aroused by a wave of apprehension. Hence, they will vote in self-defense and support the status quo to avoid being moved out. They do have a point. The housing alternatives for a public housing family are not plentiful.

What will City Hall and elected officials do? They will look for a way out. And they will find other uses for the taller high rises or have them demolished, one at a time.

Don't misunderstand me. No politician is anxious to deal with this tempestuous issue. But the writing is on the wall for the Cabrini-Green high rises. It's only a question of when their reuse or removal will begin.

Chicago Alderman Burton Natarus, whose 42nd ward covers most of the Lower North Side, flatly states that "there will be no public policy which removes blacks from the Near North Side, whether low income or middle income." Natarus' principle, however, is roomy enough to accommodate a first step which would vacate some high rises and resettle their tenants in other Cabrini-Green buildings and straightforward enough to ensure the future of the Cabrini row houses and perhaps the seven-story Cabrini buildings close to Chicago Avenue. A longtime resident of a Cabrini-Green row house endorses the strategy. She says:

We can't tear down the high rises all at once., the way they did it in St. Louis. That would produce an uprising the City couldn't control.

Let's start somewhere. Let good families in the worst high rises move into vacant apartments elsewhere in Cabrini. Stage the turnover, building by building. It may take ten years to rescue kids from the high rises. But the sooner we begin, the quicker will the kids be saved.

The CHA itself has reached, in part, the conclusion that hives of poverty and high rises with swarming children produce unhealthy and inhumane social environments. In Cabrini-Green the CHA has already vacated the apartments on the upper floors of the tallest buildings and sealed them. When inner city renovation finally lays siege to Cabrini-Green, the newcomers to the Lower North Side, many of them politically influential, will clamor for a new use for, or outright demolition of, the high rises and for the relocation of families with children. That day is not far away. In the meantime, relocation can begin immediately by emptying one high rise at a time. Tenant transfers can be started before the high rises begin collapsing on their own — beneath the weight of deferred maintenance, outrageous vandalism and structural hazards.

There are enough vacant apartments in various Cabrini-Green buildings to which the tenants remaining in the two or three tallest and worst buildings can be relocated expeditiously. If a Cabrini-Green apartment is available for each dislocated family, no household would be required to leave the project against its will. The gradual and humane relocation of households to another site in Cabrini-Green would help defuse the political pressure on City Hall to keep the housing towers.

Each existing building site is a potential oasis. When a building is torn down, the newly cleared land can then be turned over to a community-based housing group, such as the Near North Development Corporation or Atrium Village (see Chapter 11), for the construction of low-rise apartments, some of which would be rented to households from Cabrini-Green. A housing lawyer points out, for example, that the Near North Development Corporation

> located less than two blocks from Cabrini-Green has successfully rented to low- and moderate-income families. Its buildings are well maintained and recognizable as community improvements. The management has the moxie and the savvy to do the job right and to enforce high standards for those who occupy its apartments.

The CHA's willingness to confront the future of its family-occupied high rises is hobbled by two external forces over which it has little control. In addition to racial discrimination, a housing bias against families with children pervades the Chicago metropolitan area; also many suburbs oppose the entrance of low-income households, whatever their race. The removal of such barriers will strengthen the CHA's backbone and persuade it to begin relocating families with small children from its disaster-prone high rises.

Discrimination against Families with Children

Since 1970, the most persuasive argument for preserving high-rise housing is that there is no place else for the residents to go. The inability of high-rise critics to suggest such places has enabled the CHA to rationalize its hands-off policy which allows the Cabrini-Green high rises, together with their debilitating social environment, to survive into the 1980s. When various Chicago suburbs and neighborhoods refuse to accept black families or to rent to low-income households, the options of a public housing family ready to settle anywhere else are severely restricted.

The general public realizes that these high rises concentrate miserable poverty and mainly house single-parent families and unwed, pregnant teen-agers, while abetting irresponsible fathers. The Cabrini-Green high rise is increasingly seen by civic leaders as an unconscionable way of life, sustained only by federal, state and local tax dollars. The citizenry is less and less willing to tolerate the use of hard-earned tax dollars to perpetuate such conditions.

The voting public's moral indignation, however, has not yet been translated into significant action. Property owners in Chicago and the suburbs still do not comprehend how their rental practices block the avenues by which tenants routinely leave CHA projects. Escape routes from Cabrini-Green to privately owned apartments are frequently barricaded against families with children and especially against black families on public assistance.

Despite an Illinois law outlawing racial bias and another specifically prohibiting housing discrimination against families with children under age fourteen, landlords regularly slam their doors to parents with children. Managers of private rental buildings still warn applicants: "No pets, no children." Public agencies in Illinois, charged with enforcing these laws, report that complaints of discrimination against households with children almost outnumber charges of racial bias by landlords.

Opening Up the Suburbs

Furthermore, there is increased public understanding that Chicago by itself does not have the capacity to accommodate all of the poor who now live within its 228 square miles, whether they live in public housing or elsewhere. Five per cent of Chicago's population resides in CHA-owned buildings, in addition to the thousands of poor who live in privately owned housing — with or without a government subsidy. There is a growing realization that the only successful approach to housing Chicago's poor will be a metropolitan-wide strategy. It was this objective which prompted Anthony Downs, one of the nation's leading urban economists, to write his pathfinding book, *Opening Up the Suburbs*. Largely ignored when it was published in the 1970s, its relevance for the 1990s is unmistakable. Advocating the dispersal of low-income households throughout a metropolitan area, Downs' book

> focuses upon counteracting the undesirable effects caused by one deeply entrenched division: the legal and political separation between central cities and suburbs in our metropolitan areas.
>
> The most serious drawback of this division is exclusion of most poor, near-poor, and ethnic minority households from many of our suburban areas. Such exclusion helps perpetuate a host of problems by concentrating the burdens of coping with poverty inside central cities. It also prevents suburbs from achieving certain improvements in their efficiency and quality of life. . . .
>
> "Opening up the suburbs" means increasing housing opportunities in all suburban areas for low-income households and in new-growth portions of suburban areas for moderate-income households.

In the past the CHA and City Hall have been reluctant to begin vacating the shabbiest high rises and to relocate their tenants elsewhere because this would mean that Chicago's dominant political party would lose thousands of its staunchly Democratic voters. That objection can be overridden if suburban communities agree to accept their "fair" share of the metropolitan area's low-income families who now live in CHA high rises. That interurban transfer of public housing residents is already underway. In 1970, for example, the Illinois suburbs of Chicago accommodated only 5,235 subsidized housing units. By 1980, however, that number had grown to 29,463. A growing number of Cook County Democratic leaders is willing to accept the trade-off.

Since 1976 the Leadership Council for Metropolitan Open Communities has found rental apartments for nearly 3,000 CHA families (including some off the CHA waiting list) in private housing scattered throughout the Chicago metropolitan area. Sixty per cent of these apartments are located in the suburbs. Using rent subsidies supplied by the U.S. Department of Housing and Urban Development, the Leadership Council has a goal of finding privately owned apartments for 5,000 more families — at the rate of fifty a month. The count of CHA families relocated under this program thus far almost equals the number of families living legally in Cabrini-Green.

Interim Planning

Chicago can ill afford further depletion of its already inadequate supply of housing for low-income families. Can anything be done to slow down the dilapidation of CHA high rises, make their living environment more humane and heighten the responsibilities of tenants? When the CHA begins pondering the fate of its family high rises, it can take several steps which would extend their life. These steps, however, demand a fundamental change in the CHA's management philosophy, attitude and style.

From week to week the CHA is bogged down as it strives to maximize scarce resources, cope with lawsuits or ease nerve-shattering crises. Gang shootings, elevator breakdowns, frozen water pipes, unheated apartments and leaking roofs so preoccupy the CHA's daily agenda that it has thus far proved incapable of providing its own alternatives to high-rise living for families with young children. Caught in a recurring cycle of emergencies, the CHA is geared primarily to boarding up smashed windows, fixing damaged elevators or replacing broken boilers. The CHA is preoccupied, night and day, with keeping the ship afloat. It is not set up, organizationally or psychologically, to make long-term plans. Yet there are some interim steps that can be taken.

Individualizing High-Rise Public Housing

The CHA can start planning the fate of the Cabrini-Green high rises by dismantling the "project" image and syndrome. How? The CHA can treat each family individually and can give residents an address at which they will be proud to live, thus recognizing the strengths and weaknesses of each family. What the CHA has devised can be revised. Focusing on one building at a time, the CHA can take three steps.

● *Establish a separate budget* for each high rise in order to give its tenants an incentive to improve the conditions in their own building. Where tenants stop wasting energy, pay their rents on time, ward off graffiti, curb elevator vandalism, comply with high standards of housekeeping and help fill vacancies promptly, they — and their building — should benefit from the reduction in operating costs. Under the present system, however, the money saved in a "good" building is used to subsidize the "bad" buildings, i.e., those with the most broken windows, toilets or stoves, with the costliest upkeep and with the highest energy bills. Instead, whenever a high rise operates below budget, all or part of the surplus would be returned to the building for further improvments. In January of each year, the building tenant council would review a statement of the financial condition of its high rise and propose improvement priorities for the coming year. City-wide and project-wide budgets that do not individualize the income and expenditures of each building are anachronisms.

To enlist the cooperation of tenants and to generate enthusiasm among them, the CHA would have to risk rehabilitating each high rise — indeed an expensive investment of scarce resources. To ensure that this rehabilitated high rise stays in good condition after renovation, the CHA would have to implement reforms which it has hesitated to introduce in the past: guarantee high standards of tenant occupancy; upgrade day-to-day maintenance while gaining tenant assistance in the upkeep of apartments and hallways; and provide tight security in the lobbies, corridors and elevators. Furthermore, families with children would be allowed to lease only walk-up apartments on the first three floors so that youngsters would have no reason to ride the elevators. Apartments above the third floor would be rented only to the elderly or to adults without children. Were these conditions to be met, the CHA might be able to prolong the life of some high rises while it plans their eventual disposition.

● *Assign a CHA professional* who is highly motivated, adequately compensated and fully trained, to each building. That person would be required to know who lives in each apartment, to visit families in their apartments and to come to recognize them by name. The era of nameless residents would draw to a close. For all practical purposes, this CHA professional would operate as a "double agent" — not only to ensure that CHA policies are being observed but also to convey tenant complaints to the CHA management so that legitimate grievances would be adjusted quickly.

The Cabrini-Green image of a huge, monolithic development, with little differentiation among its parents and their youngsters, would start to dissolve. Once the "project facade" is removed, it will become evident that each building houses an amazing variety of inhabitants. Law-abiding families live side by side with those who hide in the shadowy world of gangs and drugs. The rate of vandalism and crime differs from high rise to high rise. Each family should be treated accordingly. In addition, each housing unit would be metered individually for heat, electricity and gas. Energy services would no longer be "free;" households that use energy economically would no longer subsidize the wastefulness of others. Were the CHA ever to individualize one of its high rises, it would have an accurate count of those who live in its properties and pay rent.

● *Forget the "Cabrini-Green" name* in all CHA publications and communications; use only the building addresses (for example, 515 West Oak Street or 1119 North Cleveland Avenue); and individualize their names as Oak Terrace, Cleveland Towers, etc. In news accounts the mass media will have to cooperate by shelving the "Cabrini-Green" stereotype and giving the person's building address instead. (In Toronto, the Canadian newspapers supply an address but do not publish the name of the housing development.) A former Cabrini-Green resident endorses this proposal:

> In the years that I lived there, I always gave 630 West Evergreen Street as my home address, whenever asked. My neighbors and I never volunteered "Cabrini-Green." Why should we? We didn't live in Cabrini-Green but on Evergreen. We could do without the stigma of that name. Cabrini-Green is a name that came from downtown. Why should we let them treat us like "project" families when we are not?
>
> Let the tenants pick the name for that building. And let the CHA consider it as scattered site housing.

There are no painless choices — for high-rise dwellers in Cabrini-Green or for CHA officials downtown. But the individualization of the high rises together with the step-by-step relocation of Cabrini-Green residents can become a prototype for renovation and reuse of other high-rise housing projects in dangerous condition.

10

An Area in Transition

*Underdevelopment today is not
a natural condition, but an
unnatural one, a social state which
is the product of history.* —Peter
Wosley, *The Three Worlds*

Throughout the first five decades of the 20th century, the Lower North Side's historic slum had been tucked safely away from public view. During the decades that followed, public attention was riveted on the migration of Chicagoans to the suburbs. By the 1960s the slum blight, hitherto confined to the Lower North Side, started spreading northward into Lincoln Park and eastward to the Gold Coast's doorstep. Throughout the 1960s and 1970s community leaders and government officials frantically built urban breakwaters to hold back the menacing tide of deterioration. They succeeded in containing the blight. A city alderman described the turnabout that took place:

> Two "urban renewal" projects (one inside the Lincoln Park community and the other next to the Gold Coast) were bitterly controversial. The city's political leadership, however, refused to budge. Protestors failed. The two projects went ahead; and they succeeded.
>
> Unbelievably, they generated a countervailing force of neighborhood revitalization. The urban revival then proceeded, block by block, to *reclaim* the turf which had earlier been inundated by blight exuding from the Lower North Side. That counterattack recoups more land each year, moving nearer and nearer to Cabrini-Green.

These two "success stories" inevitably steered City Hall's attention in the 1980s to the neighboring Lower North Side. What future did this area have as a community? Was it to be revitalized, for example, like the Lincoln Park community?

In appraising the weaknesses and strengths of the Lower North Side, it would be a colossal blunder to regard it as a community. In any urban setting, a community consists of families and individuals who occupy an identifiable territory and who share, more or less, common history, culture, religious institutions, government and mutual interests. The residents do more than share the same turf; they also enjoy some common identity and cohesiveness.

As far back as 1929, Zorbaugh had already recognized that the Lower North Side was "nondescript":

> . . .it is doubtful whether, in any proper sense of the word, the "Lower North Side" can be called a community at all. It is a region. . .remarkable for the number and kinds of people huddled and crowded together in physical proximity, without the opportunity and, apparently, with very little desire for the intimacies and the mutual understanding and comprehension which ordinarily insure a common view and make collective action possible. . . . Everywhere the old order is passing, but the new order has not yet arrived. Everything is loose and free, but everything is problematic.

These prophetic words, written fifty years ago, aptly describe the situation on the Lower North Side in the 1980s, but with three important differences. It is no longer a port of entry; there are no historic ethnic neighborhoods left to preserve; and at its center is the daunting presence of Cabrini-Green.

Since the Lower North Side is no longer a port of entry, newcomers to the city have been settling in outlying areas where new ports of entry have been opened. A real estate wizard is quick to point out, "that the suburban move isn't necessarily bad, because that's the same direction where many of the jobs are going, anyway."

No Community

In the 1980s the Lower North Side, nearly two square miles in size, survives not as a community but as a hodgepodge of more or less incompatible land uses. There are gigantic wholesale centers (like the Merchandise Mart); languishing industrial tracts (like those on Goose Island); two large housing complexes in distress (publicly owned Cabrini-Green and privately held Town and Gardens); a divinity school known world-wide (Moody Bible Institute); and a multi-national retailer (Montgomery Ward & Co.).

Despite the revitalization taking place at its southern, northern and eastern edges, the Lower North Side does not contain a single supermarket, hospital, department store, movie house or community theater. Only one franchised "fast food" outlet has survived, though several others have tried and gone bankrupt. It does not enjoy, within its boundaries, the services of a bank, drug store or post office, except those located in the Merchandise Mart, which because of their location are seldom patronized by local residents. On the other hand, no less than five currency exchanges, the "banks" traditionally used by the very poor, dot the Lower North Side. The area remains an ill-matched, splotchy weave of noisy taverns, dingy-looking grocery stores, government agencies, schools and hundreds of vacant, slum-cleared acres.

In their midst is a scattering of religious institutions: historic shrines, places of worship that once served different ethnic groups, and storefront churches which come and go. Most churches, some whose origins date back to the 19th century, are underfinanced and understaffed. Their congregations are transient and young, mostly children and mothers. Their pastors, overwhelmed by the huge cost of heat and light, scramble night and day for survival.

Here and there, one can stumble on a handsome new residential building, clean and well-scrubbed, but in the next block sidewalks look like they have been battered by a sledgehammer. Whiskey bottles litter the curbs. Street signs are missing. Sections of the Lower North Side located close to Cabrini-Green qualify as urban wilderness. The densely populated neighborhoods which for nearly a century characterized life on the Lower North Side were not replaced. Indeed, they were eviscerated to make room for Cabrini-Green.

In addition, the social architecture of a high-rise housing project for low-income families is not congenial to neighborhood growth. High transiency, conspicuous poverty, insignificant home ownership and a wasteland of vacant lots do not produce the buying power necessary to support neighborhood shops and stores. Also no positive focal point unites and rallies the residents. By itself, the Lower North Side does not contain the nutrients to nourish a distinct neighborhood identity. Under such conditions, the Lower North Side's future will not be determined by community self-improvement initiated and carried out by local residents and institutions. Its future will be engineered elsewhere, in contrast to the self-determining revitalization which now characterizes a dozen Chicago communities.*

The Erosion of the Lower North Side

The Lower North Side's future as a self-sufficient community is being eroded by the steady influx of new residents who align themselves with institutions, professional associations, shopping centers, recreational activities and workplaces based outside the area. While these newcomers live in their own homes, condominiums or townhouses or rent apartments in multi-family buildings which have been newly built or rehabbed, their loyalties are not given to the Lower North Side but go elsewhere.

As shopkeepers, restaurants, art galleries and wholesalers multiply each year, they attach themselves to neighboring areas: the Lincoln Park community, the downtown business district or the lakefront Gold Coast. They rely on the economic, social and cultural reputation of adjoining areas. Accordingly, they reject any connection to the Lower North Side, which would identify them with Cabrini-Green.

A businessman, whose family lived in the Lincoln Park community for three generations and who had monitored the Lower North Side's ups and downs for nearly fifty years, had his own version of the area's future. With a twinkle in his eye, he confided:

> The Lower North Side is a lady with a past. What will become of her with the passage of years? At this stage in her history, she stands at a crossroads, forced to choose new directions, a new way of life. The rest of the world couples her with Cabrini-Green. But she searches for a fresh identity, a name of her own. She yearns for independence — from the past and from government projects. She looks forward to becoming self-reliant and self-possessed. She could become the concubine of the Gold Coast

---

*See, for example, the author's *Reversing Urban Decline* which explains how the Edgewater and Uptown communities in Chicago overcame their urban doldrums. (Washington: National Center for Urban Ethnic Affairs, 1981)

and so gain a new identity. She could accept an offer of marriage from downtown Chicago's matchmakers. She could remain unattached and mellow as a dowager, an old maid or a streetwalker. Or she could, if she chose, vanish from the Chicago scene altogether, never to reappear.

The nagging concern about the Lower North Side's future can be illuminated by posing a set of future-oriented conclusions: (1) It has become a no man's land, vulnerable to encroachment by aggressive neighbors. (2) A bona fide community is unlikely to evolve on the Lower North Side. (3) It cannot sustain itself as a community blessed with lively private institutions and viable networks of caring neighbors. (4) Nor will the Gold Coast and the "slum" finally embrace each other, both standing comfortably under the umbrella of the Near North Side, Community Area #8.

These four conclusions are charted by the social, political and economic trends which currently shape the future of the Lower North Side. These trends apply to the larger area known as the Near North Side and to each of its two sub-sections, the lakefront Gold Coast and the Lower North Side.

Near North Side Trends

A survey of Community Area #8, known as the Near North Side, reveals five trends.

● It has been losing residents since 1950. (See Table III.)

● Its population continues to decline in the 1980s, but more slowly than in previous decades, because of spectacular residential construction near the lakefront.

● Besides the national trends of falling birth rates and smaller family sizes, the principal reason for the Near North Side's overall depopulation since 1950 has been the demolition of older residential buildings, concentrated in the Lower North Side section. Ninety per cent of the houses standing on the Lower North Side in 1930 had been demolished by 1970. They have seldom been replaced.

● Apart from the families living in Cabrini-Green Homes and the Town & Garden Apartments, childless couples where both husband and wife are gainfully employed outside the home or elderly households predominate.

● Twenty-two per cent of the Near North Side's population lived in Cabrini-Green in 1980. As the overall population of the

Near North Side grows, the proportion living in Cabrini-Green will decline.

Table III

THE NEAR NORTH SIDE AND ITS TWO
SUB-AREAS, THE LOWER NORTH SIDE AND THE
LAKEFRONT GOLD COAST: POPULATION, 1940 - 1980

Year	Near North Side	Lower North Side		Gold Coast Area*
1940	76,954	31,317	(41%)	45,637 (59%)
1950	89,196	37,616	(42%)	51,580 (58%)
1960	75,509	33,350	(44%)	42,159 (56%)
1970	70,269	27,978	(40%)	42,291 (60%)
1980	67,167	21,772	(32%)	45,395 (68%)

*The "Gold Coast" which is part of the Near North Side has shifting meanings. The name is usually given to a small exclusive section on the northeast edge of the area. On the other hand, by extension, "Gold Coast" is used to designate the entire lakefront area from LaSalle Drive east, including State Street and Michigan Avenue. The above statistics apply to the larger area. (*Source*: U.S. Bureau of the Census.)

Along The Lakefront Gold Coast

The overall trends for the Near North Side are misleading because of the striking differences between its two sub-sections. If each section is looked at separately, the divergence becomes dramatic. With regard to the lakefront Gold Coast section of Community Area #8, three trends can be identified.

● Because of tremendous commercial and residential development, the population of the lakefront section has not lost significant population. Since the 1960s the area's population began to grow steadily and will continue to do so in the 1990s.

● Its population, despite the predominance of childless couples, continues to rise as thousands of new residential units are built and occupied.

● More middle and upper income blacks keep moving into lakefront apartments where the monthly rents can be as high as $7,000. The lakefront population, racially speaking, is no longer lily-white.

In 1980 six per cent of the residents were black. The 2,500 black residents represent an 800 per cent increase since 1940. (See Table IV.)

Several decades ago the population distribution — between the Lower North Side and the Gold Coast lakefront — was more balanced. Nowadays, however, the dwellers in the lakefront area greatly outnumber the population living on the Lower North Side. The ratio is now two to one and growing greater. By sheer force of its numbers alone, the lakefront Gold Coast has begun to dominate and shape the future of the entire Near North Side. That influence becomes more significant as the Gold Coast bulges westward toward — and beyond — LaSalle Drive.

Table IV

LAKEFRONT GOLD COAST: POPULATION 1940 - 1980, COMPARED WITH CHICAGO*

| Year | Gold Coast | | | Chicago |
	Total	Black	White & Other	Total
1940	45,637	343 (1%)	45,294 (99%)	3,376,483
1950	51,580	1,106 (2%)	50,474 (98%)	3,620,962
1960	42,159	1,838 (4%)	40,321 (96%)	3,550,404
1970	42,291	1,293 (3%)	40,998 (97%)	3,369,359
1980	45,395	2,469 (5%)	42,926 (95%)	3,005,061

*Between 1950 (peak year) and 1980, the lakefront Gold Coast area's population dropped by only twelve per cent, while Chicago's population as a whole decreased by seventeen per cent. In 1950 Chicago's population had reached 3,620,962, the largest in its history, and declined thereafter. In 1950 the lakefront Gold Coast area contained 1.4 per cent of the city's residents; in 1980, 1.5 per cent. (*Source:* U.S. Bureau of the Census.)

West of LaSalle Drive

On the Lower North Side, the western section of Community Area #8, eight dramatic trends are evident.

● The depopulation of the Lower North Side has been arrested. Further losses in black residents are being offset by a return of middle class white households. (See Chapter 12.)

● The slide in the Lower North Side's white population "bottomed out" in 1980. Since then, whites have begun to return. Their number has increased and will double by 1990.

● The westward movement of households from the lakefront area across LaSalle Drive brings with it an increasing number of white households. They rent apartments rehabilitated or newly constructed since 1980.

● Despite the concentration of low-income households in Cabrini-Green, the proportion of middle-income households within the entire Lower North Side grows. (More than eighty per cent of the Lower North Side's population in 1980 lived in Cabrini-Green Homes and in Town and Gardens. Since then, however, their share of the Lower North Side's population has been decreasing.)

● The growing black population peaked in 1970; by 1980, however, it had declined by 22 per cent. It would have decreased even further had it not been for the continuing presence of Cabrini-Green's households. (See Table II in Chapter 3.)

● The number of blacks on the Lower North Side will continue to decline because of lower birth rates, more single-parent households and smaller families.

● Aside from Cabrini-Green, the population of the Lower North Side is increasingly adult, middle class and white.

● The average income of Lower North Side residents is rising because of the growing number of new middle-income residents, the majority of whom are white.

The residential development of the Lower North Side takes place side by side with commercial revitalization; "mixed use" is seen as the wave of the future. These inner-city blocks will no longer be used exclusively for commerce or government. Instead, the infusion of thousands of new housing units — the majority for middle-income households, but many for lower-income families — will guarantee that the Lower North Side's streets will accommodate pedestrian traffic days, evenings and on weekends. Theaters, drug stores and restaurants along these two-shift streets will be patronized, both day and evening, not only by suburbanites and others who commute each day to the Lower North Side to work but also by those who live there and walk to work.

New development on the Lower North Side avoids repeating the mistakes of the past. Stores and offices which stay open nine-to-five may be good for the daytime but are disasters for sidewalk activity in the evening. Similarly, huge parking lots discourage the pedestrian traffic that fosters lively, interesting and safe streets during the evening hours. On the Lower North Side a century ago, workers who were employed in the local factories lived within walking distance. As urban transportation improved, new residential areas, especially in the suburbs, were built as far away from factories and warehouses as possible. But times change and so does the taste for urban amenities. In inner city neighborhoods now undergoing rejuvenation, residential and commercial use of the land is intermixed, restoring a unique urban environment.

Counterbalancing Political Power

On three sides of Cabrini-Green the racial and economic make-up of the Lower North Side is changing. There is more racial integration and more private ownership. Sections of the area are neither all black nor all white. It is no longer certain that the Lower North Side will stay predominantly black and low-income through the year 2000; or that the social and economic cleavage between lakefront wealth and riverside poverty will widen; or that the people who currently live on the Lower North Side will continue to be short-changed while influence and power is stockpiled on the Gold Coast. The unknown factor is the future of Cabrini-Green and its residents.

The expanding population on the Lower North Side will have little impact upon the "clout" which lakefront condominium owners exert through their occupational and professional connections downtown. Setting aside those larger zones of influence, the local balance of power between the eastern and western sectors of the Near North Side will become more equal in the decades ahead. As the number of new residents who do not live in Cabrini-Green continues to rise, their votes and voices will offset the electoral power now lodged in the public housing project. When the quality of Lower North Side shops and stores improves, they will attract non-resident buyers, establishing new connections to the Chicago beyond Cabrini-Green. The area has a future but not as the Lower North Side.

11

The Bridges

*If it is possible, it can be done.
If it is impossible, it must be
done.* —Mother Cabrini

As 1990 draws near, newcomers to the Lower North Side continue to settle in the vicinity of Cabrini-Green. However, they resemble in income, education, housing style and occupation those who live in adjoining communities. The trend apparently is irreversible. More importantly, the newly arrived Lower North Siders have more empathy with their neighbors to the north and east. Newcomers to the Lower North Side keep their social, economic and political linkages to the Lincoln Park community, to downtown and to the lakefront and its Gold Coast, thus erecting two-way bridges from and to the Lower North Side. They identify with these communities rather than with the Lower North Side.

The prototype of a bridge-building institution is the local church. In urban areas of high transiency, Protestant churches are expected to follow their departing parishioners. As the people move out, the pastor abandons the church building, moves to where the congregation has gone and begins a fund-raising campaign to build a new church. Catholic churches, however, remain. As parishes they are defined geographically. Their parishioners and supporters may move out, but the pastor and his institutional network stay around to welcome the latest wave of newcomers.

LaSalle Street Church

In this respect the LaSalle Street Church is the exception to the Protestant rule and resembles more the traditional Catholic parish in the city. According to the Rev. William Leslie, senior pastor at LaSalle Street Church:

> While we commit ourselves to providing community for all those who are committed to our fellowship, we also seek to affirm the parish concept or turf principle which views as the areas of special concern all those persons and institutions within a mile radius of the church.

That one-mile radius encompasses most of the Near North Side and part of the Lincoln Park community. Within that "parish," LaSalle Street Church plays a pre-eminent role as bridge builder. No other Lower North Side church has programs which touch as many Cabrini-Green residents. At the same time, it attracts young professionals, artists, students and professors, homemakers and junior executives from elsewhere. In their "mission" statement:

> The members of the LaSalle Street Church have committed themselves to pursue a course that views our congregation as a "bridge" church with those whom our society designates as "the poor" as a special focus of concern. As a "bridge church" we view as our ideal a pluralistic and heterogenous congregation, desiring to include in our Christian community those of varying evangelical theological traditions, those of different races and those of varied social status.

It is not coincidental, but providential, that the church is strategically located on LaSalle Drive, which subdivides the Near North Side into its eastern and western sectors. A river of heavy automobile traffic, night and day, separates the two sections, but the church has learned to cross it.

When the church celebrated its 100th anniversary in 1982, a resolution adopted by the Chicago City Council took note:

> LaSalle Street Church stands in the middle like a bridge lying between the extremes of the sprawling ghetto of the west and "One Magnificent Mile" of excitement and good life along the lakefront to the east. . . .

In addition to weekly worship services, a choir and a Sunday school, the church has "ministries" for teen-agers, for school children who get onc-on-one tutoring, for senior citizens, for singles who seek counseling, for unwed mothers and for those who need legal aid. After visiting the church, Roy Larson, then religion writer for the *Chicago Sun-Times,* advised his readers:

> All ye who enter the LaSalle Street Church, check your stereo-

types at the door. . . .According to the conventional wisdom, Protestant churches flop in polyglot urban neighborhoods, young adults avoid the church en masse and evangelicals have numb social consciences. In Bill Leslie's congregation, however, . . .the embryo of hope is alive and well. It's enough to make a reserved Anglican like me shout, "Hallelujah!"

By the early 1980s, the LaSalle Street Church had become the single most influential religious institution actively shaping the Lower North Side's future.

Atrium Village

The most spectacular bridge developed by LaSalle Street Church is Atrium Village, a private housing development with 307 apartments. Its prime sponsor was LaSalle Street Church, in cooperation with three other local churches: Holy Family Lutheran, St. Matthew Methodist (both located next door to Cabrini-Green) and Fourth Presbyterian (situated on Michigan Avenue).

A fifth, St. Dominic Catholic Church, also close to Cabrini-Green, was originally a partner in the consortium of churches. Its pastor, however, was ordered to withdraw by Archbishop John Patrick Cody, although the archbishop himself at the time served on the board of directors of another corporation which was building housing south of Chicago's Loop. After Archbishop Cody's death, the pastor of St. Joseph Catholic Church, across the street from Cabrini-Green, joined the housing consortium without any objections from "downtown."

Built in 1978 on land assembled by the Chicago Department of Urban Renewal as part of its "Project Chicago-Orleans" and cleared by its bulldozers, Atrium Village occupies a seven-acre site adjacent to Cabrini-Green, which had remained vacant for nearly a decade. Conventional housing developers had avoided a site so close to Cabrini-Green. The churches, however, saw it as the ideal location because of its bridge-building possibilities. They promoted Atrium Village as the way to settle the wasteland between Cabrini-Green's public housing and the lakefront's plush condominiums and thus

> to stabilize the community between Cabrini-Green and the Gold Coast...by creating a bridge for living between the two communities.

C. William Brubaker, executive vice-president of Perkins & Will, an

architectural, engineering and planning firm, stressed the importance of its location: "Atrium Village is an amazing accomplish-
ment, a link between Cabrini-Green and the east side of the Near
North Area." In an editorial, the *Chicago Tribune* called Atrium
Village a new kind of urban housing:

> In the search for effective ways to help the poor get better housing
> without creating more monstrous public housing projects or
> urban ghettos, Chicago's planned Atrium Village. . .[was] de-
> signed to draw a mix of subsidized tenants and middle class
> renters. Its economic integration should minimize the problems
> that have plagued public housing projects. And Atrium Village's
> location should help stabilize and upgrade the Near North Side. It
> is. . .about halfway (geographically and symbolically) between
> the lakefront Gold Coast and the trouble-ridden Cabrini-Green
> housing project.

Several years after Atrium Village was occupied, its significance
was pointed up by M.W. Newman in the *Chicago Sun-Times*:

> Nobody wanted urban renewal land. . .not even for $2.50 a
> square foot. The "L" screeches by, and the Cabrini-Green hous-
> ing project is only two blocks west. Four neighborhood churches,
> joined by public and private sources, decided to build anyway.
> The result is Atrium Village, an $11 million bridge between
> Cabrini-Green and the Gold Coast two blocks east. The experts
> said it wouldn't work.

> Atrium Village now is a model of mixed-income and superbly
> managed non-profit housing. . . . Its apartments are sprinklered.
> There's a swimming pool [and tennis courts, a 24-hour doorman,
> landscaped open space, and free parking spots]. The main build-
> ing gets so much sunshine through its skylight that plants grow
> fast in the first-floor lounge.

> Poor people can live in a $400-a-month apartment at Atrium
> Village for $40 or $50, thanks to a federal rent subsidy
> program. . . . The handsome place is a bargain even for those
> paying the full price, and there are $50,000-a-year families in
> Atrium Village. "We've had less trouble here than at Gold Coast
> buildings I've managed," said Atrium Village's manager. "It's a
> hot neighborhood now," said John L. Petersen, president of
> Atrium Village. Too hot, perhaps. Housing is going up nearby on
> land that has escalated to $40 a square foot.

Atrium Village's impact upon the future of the Lower North Side
is difficult to overestimate. As a community housing development,

Atrium Village became the churches' way of achieving economic and racial integration in a no man's land lodged between social and economic extremes. A local pastor explained Atrium Village's radical aims:

> Its purpose was to bring blacks and whites together, to bring low and high income folk together from slum and Gold Coast. Atrium Village residents may be rich or poor, but they share the same attitude. They want to create a caring and loving community. The atrium architecture was chosen because it would foster community. The architecture is opposed to that realized in the Cabrini-Green *and* lakeshore high rises. Their apartments were designed for privacy, isolation, and noninvolvement. Atrium Village is pro-community and constructed in a way to nourish it. Anybody can build housing. Who will build a community?
>
> Gentrification has to come if there is to be revitalization. Displacement then follows. Atrium Village is a way of coping with the hardships that ensue. Why should upwardly mobile parishioners from Cabrini-Green be forced to move away? Why must people displaced by community improvements move out, decimating our leadership and volunteer network? Give them the opportunity to stay in the neighborhood — if that's their choice. If they want to keep their ties to our churches and schools, we need housing that will keep them around. We want, if we can, to hold that leadership in the neighborhood. Then we can stabilize our churches and provide models for other public housing residents.
>
> I know that the slums on the Lower North Side are legendary. But why should they continue for the next hundred years? I'm not an urban pessimist. We learn from the mistakes of the past. We will reclaim that land for decent housing and good neighboring.

As a housing development in what was once an urban war zone, Atrium Village is not protected by physical barriers. No moat or drawbridge which can be pulled up at night guarantees safety for residents. Atrium Village's sense of community (inside) and its architecture (outside and inside), however, are security-sensitive.

Atrium Village's Future

Atrium Village will succeed if it remains a bridge. In the eyes of its founding pastors, it will have failed if it becomes identified exclusively either with Cabrini-Green or the Gold Coast lakefront. Atrium Village was intended to be, simultaneously, an outpost for Cabrini-Green dwellers and for the lakefront affluent, to bring each group closer together. A young lawyer renting a one-bedroom apartment in Atrium Village had his own version of bridge building:

> Atrium works not because the Gold Coast's upper crust rushed over to fill it up. That did not happen. But enough middle-income, white and blue collar workers did move in — to keep the Gold Coast connection viable.

> On the other hand Atrium Village's sponsors kept their roots in, and their promises to, Cabrini-Green. Enough families moved in from the housing project to give Cabrini-Green residents some pride and hope in their "ownership" of Atrium Village. By keeping the viaduct open from the Gold Coast, Atrium Village did not become an extension of Cabrini-Green. The racial and income balance among tenants is precarious, however.

It took ten years of red tape to plan, finance, build and occupy Atrium Village, even though Crane Construction, builder of several luxury, lakefront high rises, worked with the churches as a general partner. Ever since Atrium Village was completed in 1978, its not-for-profit sponsors have been trying to buy the adjoining vacant land to erect 400 additional housing units. The fear is that the second phase may also take ten years to finish. A board member of the not-for-profit housing corporation organized by the five churches said:

> We discovered that there is no shortcut to neighborhood revitalization and better housing. If you have the patience or don't die in the meantime, persistence will pay off. I hope we can find an easier way.

Atrium Village's chances of long-term success will be enhanced if it can expand on the vacant land to its south and build more apartments. John Cordwell, an architect and urban planner who designed Carl Sandburg Village two blocks to the east, emphasized the importance of scale:

> When you're redeveloping a poverty area, you can't nibble away at it. . . . You just can't drop a few middle-income people in by parachute. . . . The question for Atrium, I guess, is whether it can fight its way back to the main bridgehead on the Gold Coast.

The first doorman at Atrium Village in 1978 sensed its historic importance. Speaking with an air of proprietorship, he said:

> This place is the Near North Side of the future. All those fellas, Arthur Rubloff and them, they're watching this place to see what happens.

Two months later, Rubloff, the Near North Side's flamboyant real estate tycoon, was quoted as saying that the demand for Near North Side housing was so great that "you can forget about Cabrini and the racial problem. That's no problem at all. From now on it is strictly a question of economics." The founding pastors of Atrium Village might not agree totally with Cordwell and Rubloff, but they fully understand that their housing development must remain a bridge that brings different groups nearer to one another. Furthermore, they see Atrium Village as a model to be replicated elsewhere in Chicago where public housing projects lie ominously close to middle class residential or commercial neighborhoods.

Other Bridge Building

Atrium Village is not the only example of bridge building between Cabrini-Green and the outside world. For example, St. Joseph Church, across from Cabrini-Green, is paired with Holy Name Cathedral located in the lakefront Gold Coast. The two churches share volunteers, resources (financial and other), personnel and a common concern for reuniting the Near North Side. Bridge building, when successful, blurs the boundaries that distinguish the two areas; it is urban ecumenism at its finest.

One of the more important viaducts is the private sponsorship of one-on-one tutoring of Cabrini-Green youngsters. In 1986 approximately 600 children were being coached once a week in reading and other skills by 600 volunteers recruited by local churches and businesses. The tutoring is often conducted away from Cabrini-Green at, for example, Fourth Presbyterian Church, the Moody Bible Institute, St. Chrysostom Episcopal Church and Montgomery Ward & Co. The youngsters are highly motivated students, anxious to extend their learning day in an environment more conducive to study than their Cabrini-Green apartment. Paradoxically, no other section of Chicago can claim to have attracted so many active volunteers as tutors.

The bridge building that goes on via regular tutoring sessions is highly personal and not easy to evaluate in view of the enthusiasm, good will and generosity of so many people. A tutor from Montgomery Ward & Co. tried to sum up what it meant to her:

> Besides the learning experience for me and my eleven-year-old girl,
> I hope that she is being exposed to a better world outside of Cabrini;
> that she is being helped to escape the project; that she becomes part
> of a helping network which can make the right connections for her;

and that she eventually becomes part of the job grapevine so that she won't be unemployed when grown up. Will tutoring be her stepladder? I hope so.

A police officer who tutors once a week added another perspective:

> The key is to reach those who are nine, ten, eleven or twelve years of age before they are romanced by the gangs. It's a constant competition for allegiance.

Greg Darneider, director of the CYCLE program for Cabrini-Green's youngsters, accented the social significance of tutoring:

> Tutoring gives competition to gangs which have carved up Cabrini-Green's turf. CYCLE is an alternative to gangs. If you enroll in a tutoring program, you get an identity. It gives you status which a gang confers, but without the hassle, extortion and violence.

Bridges are not built overnight; some are rickety and paved with surprises. When Montgomery Ward launched its tutoring program in 1965, employees were asked to volunteer. Many did, but then came the fear. To coach the children they would have to walk north across Chicago Avenue into Cabrini-Green. It was agreed, finally, that Ward's security personnel would escort them to a community room in a Cabrini-Green building. Nearly a decade later, after Montgomery Ward occupied its new twenty-six story headquarters on Chicago Avenue, a spacious cafeteria in an older building became available in the late afternoons. With its many tables, the room was ideal for one-on-one tutoring. Furthermore, many more youngsters could be tutored. Then came the crisis. This time, the Cabrini-Green youngsters were fearful, their parents worried, about safe passage. The solution was the same: supply escorts. But this time when the children walked south across Chicago Avenue to Ward's cafeteria, their escorts were older brothers or sisters, parents, aunts or uncles. Tutoring had also proved to be a two-way bridge.

Each year more Lower North Side residents attach themselves to local churches and other institutions which provide viable bridges to the world outside or which are situated outside the area. Old-time residents and new arrivals make effective use of these institutional bridges. For example, much of the one-on-one tutoring of Cabrini-Green youngsters takes place elsewhere; food shoppers on the Lower North Side trek to the supermarkets only available beyond its borders; and students travel to public and private schools in other communities.

12

Dismantling the Lower North Side

The experts are all saying that big cities
are ungovernable. What the hell do the
experts know?—Mayor Richard J. Daley

By the 1980s it was evident that programs to rebuild the Lower North Side as a distinct community, separate from its neighboring area to the east, had foundered. This realization grew slowly, through fifty frustrating years of public and private initiatives that had failed. Zorbaugh's nondescript "slum" had still not turned into a vital community. Instead a new consensus was evolving about the future of the Lower North Side. That consensus arose from a threefold experience.

● Institutional bridge building by churches, schools, housing complexes like Atrium Village, and commercial enterprises like Montgomery Ward established channels of cooperation between the Lower North Side residents and neighbors living outside its borders. As such associations multiplied they blurred the area's identity as the Lower North Side.

● As more middle-income households settled on the Lower North Side, they retained their previous connections to networks and institutions outside the area. They resisted anything that would associate their new residence with Cabrini-Green. Even as they moved physically closer to the public housing project, they strove to widen the social distance.

● An active and stable community organization depends upon the presence of a "central nervous system" which keeps the community alive and thriving. Over the decades, however, the Lower North Side proved to be so fragmented that it could not be held together under the umbrella of such an organization. Lacking a unique tradition and the driving self-interest of local churches or other institutions, each new community organization soon ran out of homegrown leaders, resources and sustaining purpose. Backers of these community organizations (a new one was organized nearly every decade) soon realized that they had little turf to defend. Transient populations, unrelenting poverty and the Cabrini-Green image made the Lower North Side unattractive to community organizers.

Cabrini-Green is too often viewed as if it can be upgraded or restored only from the outside. In Chicago, neighborhood improvement occurs only where there is an active thrust for revitalization from within as well. Where such rejuvenation is occurring, the residents are not simply recipients of revitalization but partners in the process. In the absence of grass-roots initiative, typical community organizers have bypassed the Lower North Side. For the last four decades, they have been unable to establish the power base and to uncover the local leadership that would sustain their kind of community organization.

The search, renewed each decade, for a community on the Lower North Side has proved disheartening. Since its formation in 1978, for example, the Near North Community Organization has had four executive directors and has relocated its office six times. Even though graced by boundless good will and encouraged by scores of volunteers, the NNCO leadership has been unable to cement a common ground between the residents who live in Cabrini-Green and their neighbors on the Lower North Side. Only some churches have established such a common ground.

Dismembering the Lower North Side

By 1980 the absence of a genuine community of interest and a shared history among Lower North Siders had left the area vulnerable to colonization by more prosperous neighbors. Such confiscation of Lower North Side territory was hastened by the new arrivals to the Lower North Side. Increasingly, they differed in race and income from old-time residents. More of them were white, and whether black or white they earned higher incomes.

Since the area suffered from civic neglect, its recently settled residents did not discourage empire builders interested in staking a claim to sections of the Lower North Side. Who were the encroachers? Some were City Hall planners; others represented the communications and promotion industries. What did they do? In an imperialistic manner, they seized portions of Lower North Side territory and incorporated them into larger business zones or quasi-public districts. These new affiliations not only set off the new middle-income residents from Cabrini-Green but also bracketed them with other communities of interest.

The secret is finally out. In the 1980s it is clear that there no longer is a Lower North Side; its territory can not, and will not, be defined or defended. The geographic dismantling of the Lower North Side now proceeds from all directions, its boundaries renegotiated by municipal planners, real estate developers, mapmakers, business groups and bankers. Its more desirable acres have been reclaimed and assigned to economic and political interests whose home base is elsewhere.

Chicago is served, for example, by nineteen neighborhood telephone directories, but the Lower North Side has no directory of its own. From the north, a "Lake View" directory makes off with the Lower North Side's upper section (above Division Street), while from the south a *Chicago Visitors Guide and Downtown Directory* annexes the Chicago River's north bank, the Merchandise Mart and nearby properties. The remainder of the Lower North Side, containing most of Cabrini-Green, can not be found in any neighborhood telephone directory. Such are the marketing priorities of Illinois Bell Telephone Company and the telephone books' publisher, the Reuben H. Donnelley Corporation. Residents of the Lower North Side who find their names in another neighborhood's directory do not protest the dislocation; they are instead delighted to discover their new community affiliation.

Chicago magazine's 1983 *Guide to Chicago*, publicized as "the most complete guide to the city and its neighborhoods," disregards Cabrini-Green and the Lower North Side. The *Guide* slices off two small parts, assigning one to the Lincoln Park community and the other to a "North of the River" area which ends where Cabrini-Green begins.

When tourists visit the Sears Tower, the tallest building in the world, and go up to its skydeck 103 floors above ground, they are given a map to help them view the city. That map highlights many Lower North Side institutions, including Carl Sandburg Village, but ignores Cabrini-Green, leaving a noticeably blank space on the map. One visitor asked:

> Is this because Cabrini-Green is off-limits to visiting dignitaries and other tourists? Or is the mapmaker a Chicago booster who is ashamed to admit it has a Cabrini-Green?

These are not trivial questions. In 1983 the chief executive officer of a giant U.S. corporation, based in Chicago, arranged a visit to the Lower North Side. Why? He chaired the advisory board of a Christian youth organization with a branch in Cabrini-Green. If he expected staff and volunteers to work in Cabrini-Green, why should it be off-limits for him? His associates and the corporate lawyers were astounded. Cabrini-Green was dangerous, they insisted. He rejected their pleas not to go. Aghast, they insisted that he clear his visit with the insurance company to ensure that he would be protected. After checking his insurance coverage, the corporate head attended the youth meeting and returned, undamaged, to his executive suite downtown.

Planners at Play

City Hall planners had never given the Lower North Side high priority. They were reluctant to confront alternatives to high-rise public housing. For them it was too volatile a political issue. Furthermore, resolving other urban problems, such as the declining health of Chicago's downtown, seemed less overwhelming and more amenable to public/private planning.

By the late 1960s it was evident that the introduction of high-rise public housing for low-income families had been the most disastrous event in 20th century Chicago. The City's planning department, however, continued to skirt the issue. Its 118-page *Comprehensive Plan of Chicago,* released in 1966, contained three innocuous paragraphs about existing public housing and the Chicago Housing Authority.

To decentralize planning, that 1966 plan divided the city into sixteen "development areas." One of the sixteen was a new eleven-square mile "central area" from the lake west to Ashland Avenue and from North Avenue south to the Stevenson Expressway. These boundaries embraced all of the land which made up the "old Chicago'' incorporated as a City in 1837 and which is today the vital center of the city's commerce and government. (See map.)

With heavy prodding and funding from the Chicago Central Area Committee (the planning watchdog on behalf of downtown business), the City's plan for the development of the central area finally appeared in 1973. Called *Chicago 21* (planning for the 21st century), the plan brought the Lower North Side and Cabrini-Green into the central area. Cabrini-Green was listed as one of the plan's five "critical priorities." It would be improved, the plan promised, radically enough "to serve as a pilot program for public housing throughout the city." The promises were short-lived, as the real agenda of City Hall and downtown business leadership soon emerged. It was not Cabrini-Green.

It became clear that Cabrini-Green was really a low priority when the City of Chicago and the Chicago Central Area Committee in 1983 *jointly* proposed a second and preliminary plan for the central area. This time, however, the Cabrini-Green section was amputated from the central area and not even mentioned. This glaring omission meant that Cabrini-Green was no longer a "critical priority." Radical improvements proposed a decade earlier had not been implemented nor had their highly publicized objectives been achieved.

A downtown real estate broker who had meticulously compared the two plans explained why City Hall and the Chicago Central Area Committee chose to embrace Cabrini-Green in 1973 and then to exclude it from the same "central area" in 1983:

> The latest plan is far more honest. Cabrini-Green isn't even noted despite the fact that the earlier *Chicago 21* plan called attention to Cabrini in twenty-two different places. That 1973 plan didn't mean what it said nor did it say what it meant. Neither City Hall nor the downtown business establishment was ready to deal with Cabrini. They still aren't.

> In 1973 the private and public planners were more preoccupied with revitalizing State Street and with flooding the central area with middle- and upper-income residents. Those were the real priorities. Cabrini-Green was highlighted in the plan (1) because it was already on the central area map which had been published seven years earlier; (2) because everybody genuinely *hoped* that conditions at the housing project would improve; and (3) because the planners did not want to be criticized for slighting the

project's notorious problems. Don't underappreciate the power of the Chicago Central Area Committee. It holds the copyright to the 1983 plan, even though it was released jointly by the City and the Committee.

Were the Chicago Central Area Committee ultimately to restore the Cabrini-Green section to an updated version of its 1983 plan, Cabrini-Green would still receive low priority.

While Cabrini-Green was being expunged from the official central area plan, the City's planning department published an updated "comprehensive plan" for the entire city, calling it *Chicago 1992*. This 160-page plan, like the earlier comprehensive plan for Chicago in 1966, made only passing reference to the Chicago Housing Authority and to its "modernization program," described as a "massive effort" to rehabilitate 30,000 CHA apartments so that they would be "suitable for occupancy." Nothing more was said. A former city planner tried to explain:

> Though hard to justify, City Hall's position is understandable. Why would city planners take on the CHA, another public agency? That would be trespassing. It seemed wiser to leave that "hot potato" — and the blame — with the CHA.
>
> Why would anyone want to touch the prickliest of urban questions: what does CHA do with the families that now inhabit the high rises? Where would they go? What neighborhood or suburb would welcome them?
>
> It is always safer for planners to avoid questions for which they have no answer.

The latest downtown planning decisions undermined any future for the Lower North Side as a community on its own. Nearly half of the Lower North Side had been quietly attached to Chicago's central business district. Cabrini-Green and the residential sections south of the Lincoln Park community were meticulously inserted into a new North Neighborhood Planning District. City maps and those of the Chicago Central Area Committee were once again redrawn to make the latest annexation "official." The dismantling of the Lower North Side had begun. More importantly, no protest was heard from the Lower North Side.

River North, the 1980s

The southwestern section of the Lower North Side immediately north and east of the Chicago River was steadily being incorporated into the central business district. It soon flaunted a community organization. Its founders, who named the area "River North" in the 1980s, stated:

> The purpose of the River North Association is to promote River North's aesthetic development, serve as City Hall's liaison for neighborhood problems, initiate special events and foster a sense of community. . . .the association has coordinated a tree and sidewalk replacement project with City officials, spring-cleaned the streets and windows, compiled a source and service directory, hosted a variety of social functions, generated print publicity and dressed the streets with colorful banners.

River North's publicists promoted it as "Chicago's creative community" because it had lured designers, architects, photographers, graphic artists, gallery owners, antique dealers and even the Chicago City Ballet.

A remarkable change was underway in the 1980s. At the turn of the century, the area, now called River North, had been a major warehouse and manufacturing district. In subsequent decades the area declined. "For Rent" and "For Sale" signs not only proliferated but also hung for decades. Eventually, the urban pioneers arrived in the late 1970s, enticed by the lower rentals in an area close to the Loop and to the publishing, advertising and public relations firms in the Michigan Avenue corridor.

As River North, it had finally become an area of historic preservation. What gave it special character was the predominance of industrial loft buildings, built in the early 1900s when construction standards were high and building costs were modest. Today a renovated six-story factory building with fifteen-foot ceilings, hardwood floors and open floor space may house restaurants, advertising agencies, law offices, condominium loft residences and furniture show rooms. Some newly opened offices and galleries are located only two blocks from Cabrini-Green. An owner of a fifth floor loft assessed the inner city dynamics:

> Where else can you find such architectural diversity? Nine-foot windows? Exposed brick walls? Here one can afford to rent or buy unobstructed interiors which can be custom designed, for working or living space, to suit the tastes of the occupant.

> Solid, brick buildings, once used for light industry and manufacturing, are being salvaged, not destroyed.

Of course River North is addicted to promotional hyperbole. That's understandable. The real estate pessimists who once owned these River North properties couldn't do anything with them. We bring them back to life. Allow us to celebrate a bit, even if, at times, we overdo it.

In the middle 1980s River North banners, flapping in the wind, were hung on light poles across the street from Cabrini-Green. These banners, like those of explorers and conquerors in other places and earlier times, laid claim to a large section of what once had been known as the Lower North Side. River North's allegiance, however, was to the lakefront Gold Coast and to the downtown business district.

Most threatened by the resurgence of River North is the shrinking population of homeless drifters who once peopled the area's "skid row." The taverns and rooming houses which they frequented are being nudged out by graphic art studios, law offices, new office buildings and refurbished loft buildings. Symbolizing the change is the tension, for example, between River North's real estate entrepreneurs and St. Francis Center's "dining room" on Kinzie Street (just north of the Chicago River). Since 1978 the center has served free meals, noon and evening, to some 500 guests daily. The center, run by volunteers and Franciscans from St. Peter Church located downtown, fills a real need as evidenced by the large numbers of the hungry who line up each day for a meal. Those lines inevitably produce friction. A Franciscan volunteer explains:

> Some neighboring merchants and professionals have been sympathetic. We've tried to work with them and respond to complaints about some of our guests who turn out to be drunks, panhandlers, loiterers or litterers. Other storekeepers press us to move so that our guests won't scare away their customers.

The conflict between St. Francis Center and neighboring businesses is not likely to subside as long as River North area prospers.

The Industrial and Commercial Corridor

The western border of the River North area is the North Branch of the Chicago River. Along both sides of the North Branch stretches a four-mile long industrial and commercial corridor which is also the western limit of both the Lower North Side and the Lincoln Park communities. The warehouses and manufacturing plants which line the riverbanks or lie on Goose Island once relied heavily on the waterway for moving their goods. As rail, road and air transport became available, the riverfront lost the advantage of its strategic location, and the aging, riverside industries suffered. Competition from modern industrial plants located elsewhere in the Chicago metropolis also hastened the corridor's decline. Ever since, the owners of underused or empty factories, vacant lots and deteriorating buildings have searched for a more prosperous future. Since the Great Depression, successful new businesses have been scattered and few.

Despite decades of apparent failure, the future of this historic, industrial corridor is slowly being shaped in its southernmost mile. Here new commercial developments (new hotels, the Apparel Center and the sports-oriented East Bank Club) are springing up along the river moving closer to Montgomery Ward & Co., whose influential presence helps anchor the new ventures. The move in 1982 of the *Chicago Tribune*'s printing and circulation operations from Michigan Avenue to a gigantic plant on Chicago Avenue was almost as significant as the opening of the Merchandise Mart in 1930. The modern $186 million newspaper plant was built on a twenty-one acre site hugging the North Branch along its west bank.

While this new commercial expansion was taking place at the southern end of the Chicago River's North Branch, efforts were also underway to upgrade the river's industrial corridor farther north. For this purpose the New City YMCA organized a Local Economic and Employment Development Council in 1982. The Council sought to conserve present jobs and to attract new industry in order to expand job opportunities for local residents. To realize these goals the Council established an industrial service area which takes in the westernmost section of the Lower North Side, including Cabrini-Green. In addition, a large portion of that industrial service area was added in 1984 to Enterprise Zone 4, a larger area designated by the City and State as distressed economically and thus eligible for tax incentives to spur business revitalization. These two new service districts aimed to revive the industrial section of the Lower North Side as part of the revitalization of the river's larger industrial corridor. In drawing their new boundaries, however, these districts absorbed the western sector of the Lower North Side, dismantling it even further.

Westward, ho!

Ever since the 1920s merchants, hoteliers and developers had concentrated their attention and investment along Michigan Avenue and the adjoining lakefront area. In the 1970s, as Michigan Avenue's land costs and office rentals escalated beyond the reach of many buyers and renters, they began investigating properties to the west — looking toward the Lower North Side. The Greater North Michigan Avenue Association soon designated this area as its "western sector." A GNMAA member offered this analysis:

> The western sector was seen only as an appendage to Michigan Avenue. Some called it the backyard. Others saw it as the "wild west," a frontier to be explored, perhaps, but not to be settled. You can be sure that the GNMAA's first thoughts were on the Magnificent Mile. The western sector was an afterthought.

In 1973 the weekly *Real Estate Advertiser* described, from a realty broker's point of view, the potential of the so-called "western sector":

> It is doubtful that any city in the world is so blessed with expansion room as Chicago. . . .one area remains with no planned development and that area is north of the Loop and west of Michigan Avenue. . . . While Michigan Avenue grows as a fashionable shopping boulevard, the area westward remains stagnant and rundown. . . .

> Meanwhile, future gold for Chicago developers is west of the [Magnificent] Mile and lies waiting to be tapped. . . . [The] west is open for development. . . .

Franklin and Irene McMahon were early purchasers of a residential condominium on the Lower North Side, six blocks west of Michigan Avenue. As a condominium owner on the lower north "frontier," Mrs. McMahon offered still another perspective:

> The Lower North Side is regarded as the backside of Michigan Avenue, the Magnificent Mile. That backside, however, is becoming smaller and smaller as the affluence of the lakefront Gold Coast creeps westward to the Moody Bible Institute and beyond, reaches the loft area north of the Merchandise Mart and encounters Atrium Village.

By 1980 Mrs. McMahon's hinterland was no longer an urban frontier safe only for explorers, discoverers and other risk takers. The settlers had also arrived. In that year Stephanie Fuller, realty writer for the *Chicago Tribune,* described the land-office frenzy moving westward:

> It's almost as if Chicagoans of today are listening to Horace Greeley saying: "Go west, young man," when you consider the "Westward, ho" movement currently afoot in the city. Due to the high cost of condominium living along the lakefront and the high costs of rents in the same area, Chicagoans are striking for less expensive pastures. Some are moving just west of Michigan [Avenue], while others are becoming urban pioneers in heretofore non-residential neighborhoods. . .that are becoming revitalized in a torrent of rehabilitation.

Table V

THE AREA BETWEEN LASALLE DRIVE AND
FRANKLIN STREET, FROM THE CHICAGO RIVER
TO NORTH AVENUE: POPULATION BY RACE, 1960 - 1980*

Year	Total	Black	White & Other
1960	11,275	4,165 (37%)	7,110 (63%)
1970	5,952	2,446 (41%)	3,506 (59%)
1980	4,791	1,227 (26%)	3,564 (74%)

*This fourteen-block strip lies inside the eastern border of the Lower North Side, which is undergoing revitalization. During this twenty-year period, the area's black population declined seventy-one per cent, while white residency only decreased fifty per cent. (*Source:* U.S. Bureau of the Census).

To encourage the westward movement Alderman Burton Natarus, whose 42nd Ward embraces all of the Lower North Side, persuaded the Chicago City Council in 1980 to change the name of LaSalle, north of the river, from "Street" to "Drive." Why did he take this step? Natarus replied:

> The older buildings along LaSalle are being restored. "Drive" is classier and reflects better the residential character of LaSalle north of the river. LaSalle Drive gives the street the near-boulevard status it deserves.

The new residential construction and rehabilitation taking place along the Lower North Side's eastern border forecast similar, long-term trends for the entire area. In the strip from the river to North

Avenue (see Table V), fourteen blocks long and two blocks wide, the overall population between 1960 and 1980 dropped fifty-eight per cent. But the proportion of whites continued to increase. The U.S. Census data in Table V for this strip are already out-of-date as new residential buildings proliferate. Since 1980 several new housing developments have been built and occupied. Others have been refurbished. New and rehabilitated buildings accommodate more than 1,000 apartments, their occupants racially diverse though chiefly white. The block-by-block revitalization proceeds without fanfare because the new housing construction uses vacant land cleared years before or involves the demolition only of commercial structures.

As the residential revitalization moves westward within the northern tier of the Lower North Side, it will join up with the new housing built by the Near North Development Corporation. The NNDC is a homegrown enterprise fostered by the neighboring Olivet Community Center and led by William Moorehead, a local resident. Since 1977 the NNDC has built 268 housing units for black families of low and moderate income. The NNDC's housing complex occupies a ten-acre tract made available by the City's Department of Urban Renewal, and it represents a triad of smaller developments: Evergreen-Sedgewick Apartments, Evergreen Tower and Evergreen Terrace. They were built with Cabrini-Green looming in the background. They sparkle as community improvements, attractive and well maintained. They have halted the area's downward slide and have not been swallowed up by the surrounding blight.

Moorehead, manager of the buildings, explains why his rental experience has been so successful:

> We ask people to present their case for living here.
>
> People get the idea that anyone who applies here is supposed to be accepted, because it's subsidized housing. But we have a commitment to maintain sound and decent housing. I personally interview all qualified applicants, and we use home visits to check out their housekeeping habits [before renting them an apartment]. We enforce management rules and won't hesitate to put out troublemakers.
>
> We're an oasis in a bleak desert. We put a lot of effort into maintaining the property and running a secure project.

In the future the NNDC expects to build or rehabilitate several hundred additional apartments. Like Atrium Village, the Evergreen housing triad minimizes displacement and offers local residents a chance to stay in the neighborhood if they wish. It demonstrates once again that inner city revitalization can readily accommodate modest amounts of federally subsidized housing.

The growing amount of good, affordable housing available on the Lower North Side increases the number of residents living close to Cabrini-Green. Such proximity, however, has done little to remove the social and economic barriers that separate Cabrini-Green from the rest of the area. Instead, the business, political, cultural and social activities of the new residents steer them in another direction —away from Cabrini-Green.

'Lincoln Park South'

In the early 1960s North Avenue had been transformed into a "Berlin Wall" running east and west and segregating the Lower North Side from the Lincoln Park community. It divided Lincoln Park's whites from the Lower North Side's blacks. By the 1980s, however, North Avenue had changed; the racial barrier had begun to dissolve. A Lincoln Park resident noted the difference:

> The visage of North Avenue is radically different from what it was twenty years ago. Gone are the dingy storefronts, the boarded up stores. Instead there are good-looking stores, a clean street and newly built housing. North Avenue's recovery is amazing. It shows what intensive care by the Chicago Department of Urban Renewal and private entrepreneurship, working together, can accomplish. North Avenue is not only a viable shopping strip but an interracial street as well.

As North Avenue's "invisible" wall crumbled, more blacks could be found in Lincoln Park and more whites on the Lower North Side. The two-way crossing was engineered by (1) public schools in search of racial integration; (2) institutions seeking a location where they could simultaneously serve clients of lower and higher incomes; and (3) homeowners who took advantage of a now more hospitable racial climate.

In the late 1960s two public high schools served the Lincoln Park community and the Lower North Side. The two schools were separated by more than geography. The student body at Waller High School, located in the Lincoln Park community, had become predominantly black. The student population at Cooley Vocational High School, situated in the Lower North Side, was solidly black; most of its students came from Cabrini-Green. Neither school was seen as college preparatory. Each came to be regarded as a "blackboard jungle." A PTA leader, with some exaggeration, summed up the situation:

> Kids who can read go to Waller. Those who can't read go to Cooley. And good students go to private or parochial schools.

Whether black or white, more middle-income families with children would ensure the revitalization of the Lincoln Park community, but such families were reluctant to move in. Families already residing there boycotted both high schools. They sent their youngsters to private schools or enrolled them in public schools elsewhere.

With pressure from parents, community activists, the federal government, the Chicago Department of Urban Renewal and local officials, the Chicago Board of Education resolved to upgrade the schooling and to attract more white students. To achieve these objectives, the board opted for bridge building between the troubled high rises in Cabrini-Green and the restored Victorian houses in the Lincoln Park community. The objective was a better racial balance between black and white students.

New School in a New Building

After a decade of controversial planning, the Chicago Board of Education decided to demolish the run-down building which harbored Cooley High School and to erect a modern building to house the Near North Career Magnet School. On the eve of the opening of the renamed high school in 1979, the Rev. McKinley Franklin, former pastor of St. Matthew United Methodist Church (located within shouting distance of Cabrini-Green), exulted:

> The old Cooley is dead. We buried it. Cooley was symbolic of mediocrity and poor performance. It was shameful to call Cooley a vocational school. We practically had no curriculum at Cooley. When students came out, they weren't prepared to go any place. . . .
>
> The new school, with a new name, will have tremendous offerings and attract students from all areas of the city. With a high caliber of teachers, administrators and programs, the school will transcend the psychological barriers associated with North Avenue and become integrated.

To increase the chances of improved education and greater racial balance, the Near North Career Magnet School was located closer to North Avenue but still on the Lower North Side. The magnet was a new $8 million building where course offerings were available in landscaping, hotel and restaurant management, graphic arts and auto mechanics. To ensure a racial balance, the Chicago Board of Education sought to limit black enrollment to approximately seventy per cent. The Near North Side Career Magnet High School opened with a student population that included Hispanics, other whites and Orientals, even though blacks were a sizable majority. Its predecessor, Cooley Vocational High School, had an enrollment that was almost 100 per cent black. (See Table VI.)

Five years later, the past and future of the Near North Career Magnet High School were assessed by McKinley Franklin who earlier had led the community campaign for a new high school. He said:

> So far, the Near North Career Magnet School is an educational success, a sparkling improvement over the old and depressing vocational school which was torn down.

> The racial balance is still precarious. Despite predictions to the contrary by educational pessimists, Near North has not only attracted black students but whites, Hispanics and Asians as well. What is the explanation? It is Near North's special curriculum and new image.

New School in an Old Building

In the Lincoln Park community, about the same time, community leaders and the Chicago Board of Education concocted a different strategy for Waller High School's future. Formerly, it had been one of Chicago's superior schools. What did the board do? They preserved the building erected in 1900 but changed its name to Lincoln Park High School. New talent and additional money was allocated to the school's band and chorus, converting them into new sources of community pride. Two million dollars were spent to revamp the inside of the building, remove grafitti and spruce up the exterior. A parent who watched the renovation expressed her approval:

> The physical improvements may be cosmetic. So what? The building finally looks like a real high school. There's a new school spirit inside. Previously that place had stood out like the last battered building in a war zone.

More importantly, the school's leadership promoted its specialized programs in arts, humanities and science, along with the core curriculum. How successful was the metamorphosis at Lincoln Park High? In 1983 *Time* magazine singled it out as an

> inner-city school with an irresistible claim to academic excellence. . . . It has a school of science with college-level courses in biochemistry, a school of languages that offers French, German, Italian and Spanish, and a school of arts that offers everything from the Stanislavsky acting method to Baroque music. This year there were 200 applicants for thirty places in Lincoln Park's International Baccalaureate program, an academically demanding two-year curriculum. . . . Says Stephen Ballis, an insurance executive and neighborhood parent: "This used to be a half-filled building, isolated from the community. Now it's overcrowded. Excellence and the expectations of excellence are contagious."

Table VI

NEAR NORTH CAREER MAGNET AND LINCOLN PARK
HIGH SCHOOLS, ENROLLMENT BY RACE,
1970, 1983 and 1984

School	Total	White	Black	Hispanic	Other
Near North*					
1970	560	0 (0.0%)	555 (99.1%)	5 (0.9%)	0 (0.0%)
1983	1026	55 (5.4%)	842 (82.1%)	90 (8.8%)	39 (3.8%)
1984	1073	78 (7.3%)	899 (83.8%)	65 (6.1%)	31 (2.8%)
Lincoln Park					
1970	1908	293 (15.4%)	969 (50.8%)	614 (32.1%)	32 (1.7%)
1983	1579	528 (33.4%)	778 (49.3%)	205 (13.0%)	68 (4.3%)
1984	1504	545 (36.2%)	698 (46.4%)	181 (12.1%)	80 (5.3%)

*The 1970 enrollment figures for Near North Career Magnet High School are for the high school it replaced, Cooley Vocational. Lincoln Park High School was previously Waller High whose proportion of black students peaked at 74.2 per cent in 1978. (*Source:* Chicago Board of Education: Racial/Ethnic Survey—Students, 1970, 1983 and 1984.)

The Chicago Board of Education's strategy to establish educational bridges across North Avenue succeeded in minimizing the striking racial differences between the Lower North Side and the Lincoln Park communities. Each with a new name and image, the two high schools are five blocks apart. One is located south of North Avenue, the other to the north. Between them, they help define a demilitarized, interracial zone which de-emphasizes the former barrier of North Avenue. Today as they walk north to classes at Lincoln Park High School, no less than 100 students from Cabrini-Green pass Hispanic and other white students headed south for classes in the Near North Career Magnet High School.

In the 1960s race and class consciousness had together erected formidable barriers to human interchange between the Lincoln Park and Lower North Side communities. Twenty years later, that racially divisive line down the middle of North Avenue had been hurdled. In the 1980s social commerce could proceed more normally. With a racial truce in place, the symbolic stockades built by economic class seemed less necessary and were gradually being removed. As the risk of racial conflict subsided, upwardly mobile blacks and whites discovered that they had economic, community and political interests which brought them together. They no longer needed North Avenue's invisible wall to ensure their safety and security. After all, they shared the same police and school districts and lobbied the same elected officials who represented them in Springfield, Illinois or Washington, D.C. Their mutual concerns found common outlets.

As its racial barriers were penetrated, North Avenue was crossed in both directions. Middle-income blacks bought or rented housing in the Lincoln Park community north of North Avenue. Some middle-income whites returned to the Lower North Side where they purchased property, rehabilitated it and moved in — on the south side of North Avenue.

For would-be Lincoln Parkers who could not afford or find a house in the Lincoln Park community, the area just south of North Avenue became a new urban frontier. They could settle there and keep their association to the Lincoln Park community. That borderland offered lower housing prices, but because it also conjured up danger, uncertainty and fear, the Lincoln Park connection was reinforced. One such urban pioneer, when asked where he lives, replied: "In Lincoln Park." He then explained:

> Saying Lincoln Park tells somebody that it is the community with which I want to identify and best conveys information about where I am located. Had I said, "Lower North Side," nobody would know where that was. Anyhow, who decreed that 100

yards south of North Avenue can't be considered part of Lincoln Park? By itself, my block is nondescript. Why shouldn't we try giving it some of Lincoln Park's character? You won't find any wolves or grizzly bears on my street. And I use its sidewalks to go to nearby stores.

Some of my neighbors, when asked where they live, choose the Near North Side; they prefer to swing with the glitter and glamor of Lake Shore Drive. I feel more at home with the residential stability and sense of community that Lincoln Park promises.

You can't say that Lincoln Park is annexing the northern edge of the Lower North Side. That's a problem that Lincoln Parkers would love to avoid. But they can't avoid it. Accommodations are underway which, in the long run, will make both sides of North Avenue a commercial and residential part of the Lincoln Park community. The Lower North Side is being nibbled away. And nobody is complaining.

Extending Lincoln Park

Almost simultaneously in the late 1970s and early 1980s, business leaders, school boards, government officials and directors of youth-serving agencies ventured to locations south of North Avenue so that they could accommodate both blacks and whites on a neutral turf.

● St. Joseph Hospital, located in the northeast corner of the Lincoln Park community near Lake Michigan, opened the Seton Medical Center on the south side of North Avenue. The hospital's new outpost became a bridge from the Lincoln Park community to the Lower North Side. Subsequently, Robert Cross in the *Chicago Tribune Magazine* etched the significance of the place and the service:

> St. Joseph [Hospital] itself stands on Lake Shore Drive, but Seton (named for the first native-born American saint) has been placed at 711 West North Avenue, at the very point where cushy Lincoln Park scuffs its Guccis on mean pavement surrounding the Clybourn subway station. Seton. . .opened on land cleared by federally subsidized bulldozers, so that nearby residents — poor and wealthy alike — would have the services of primary-care physicians and so that young doctors in that specialty would have an "inner city" setting where they could learn how to set up an effective urban family practice. . . . Patients. . .make appointments and must pay whatever their wallet or poverty program will

bear. . . . Before Seton came along the residents nearby had a difficult time finding doctors of their own.

The $3.2 million medical center houses more than twenty physicians who practice in its private offices and the clinic. The doctors make house calls. In its unique location, the Seton Medical Center treats patients who live on either side of North Avenue, thus turning out to be another bridge-building institution.

● For more than a century, the Young Men's Christian Association of Metropolitan Chicago operated from a headquarters in downtown Chicago. With a 1983 budget exceeding $35 million and with a staff of 1,400 working in centers throughout the Chicago area, the YMCA was a leader among the city's agencies providing social service. In an unprecedented move, the YMCA closed down its central downtown office in 1983 and reopened it in the Brooker Center, a new two-story building on North Avenue next door to the Seton Medical Center.

Adjoining the YMCA headquarters at its new location was the newly constructed New City YMCA, with an olympic-size swimming pool, gymnasium, day care center, classrooms, outdoor track, fitness center and community meeting rooms. It replaced the old Isham YMCA whose membership, in recent decades, had become overwhelmingly black and poor. With its new name, the New City YMCA was designed and located to achieve racial and economic integration among its users. John Root, former president of the Metropolitan YMCA, viewed the New City YMCA as a bridge builder:

> We chose this location to serve mothers and their children from Cabrini-Green, residents from Lincoln Park, and neighborhood businessmen trying to revive the industrial corridor along the North Branch of the Chicago River. The New City YMCA is doing just that. We have several hundred dues-paying members who live in Cabrini-Green.

> This YMCA is important. The last "Y" built in the city was finished in the 1950s. We wanted the New City YMCA to be a community-based institution and to have a positive impact upon the future of this inner city community. The new "Y" is a catalyst to bring everything — and everybody — together.

Stevenson Swanson, a reporter for the *Chicago Tribune,* referred to the site of the New City YMCA as

the near North Side's demilitarized zone. To the north is the predominantly white, middle class Lincoln Park neighborhood. To the south is the gargantuan Cabrini-Green public housing complex. To the west is an old industrial section hanging on for dear life. To the east is the affluent Gold Coast.

What was the result? According to Margaret Harrigan, the local school superintendent in the early 1980s:

> The coming of the YMCA in the 1980s turned the area [just south of North Avenue, east of Halsted Street and southeast of the subway station] into a new urban plaza.

It was a spectacular convergence of private and public institutions: four new buildings (the two YMCA structures on a fourteen-acre site, the family medical center and the new public high school). They bordered the Thomas Flannery Apartments (two CHA high rises for the elderly) and the Sojourner Truth Elementary School. Their combined presence created an oasis that attracted people from different races and varying economic groups during the day and evening. The new urban plaza had minimized, once again, the historic importance of North Avenue as a dividing line not to be crossed racially or economically.

The convergence centered around a transportation hub at the intersection of North Avenue, Halsted Street and the diagonal Clybourn Avenue. Here was a subway station for rapid transit trains running north and south. The trains ran below, the buses above. Their riders were local residents or those who worked in the surrounding blocks but lived elsewhere. A professional on the staff of the YMCA noted the change:

> Once it was very clear to me that I worked on the Lower North Side. Now I'm not that sure. Has this section been blended into the Lincoln Park community? On the other hand, we seem to be closer than ever to the warehouses and industries near Goose Island. You can see the change during the rush hours at the subway station; more and more of the riders are white.

> Old boundaries, ancient barriers are fading away. We're no longer, it seems, off-limits to anyone. Only muggers and drug pushers are not welcome — whatever their race.

● The busy transit center was not generated solely by government agencies and not-for-profit institutions. In the early 1980s, for example, the new urban plaza acquired a new neighbor to its west: a giant, automated furniture store, called Homemakers, hitherto operating only in the suburbs. For its fourth location, Homemakers opted for the Lower North Side. There it took over a manufacturing plant which once had employed as many as 2,000 workers, had built jukeboxes and vending machines but had gone bankrupt in the late 1970s. The new Homemakers store was geared to young, upwardly mobile customers, even though the owners were in their third generation of management as the John M. Smyth family.

● Signs of change could be found elsewhere. Commercially and residentially, the south side of North Avenue located on the Lower North Side began to resemble the area on the other side of the avenue identified with the Lincoln Park community. The Lincoln Park Chamber of Commerce's headquarters lay south of North Avenue, the southern boundary of Lincoln Park. Concluding that it had accomplished its twenty-year mission in the Lincoln Park community, the City's Department of Urban Renewal closed its office which had been situated south of North Avenue. The Lincoln Park Conservation Association had business memberships from south of North Avenue, as did the Old Town Triangle Association, a neighborhood group representing the southeast section of the Lincoln Park community. The bylaws of the Lincoln Park Conservation Association establish Division Street, four blocks south of North Avenue, as the community organization's southern boundary. Thus the Lincoln Park Community is spilling south into what once was the Lower North Side.

Bidding the Lower North Side Goodbye

The steady disappearance of the Lower North Side, as an identifiable piece of Chicago geography, as a recognizable community or as a state of mind, cannot be attributed solely to changing attitudes among its new inhabitants. As land values, building prices, taxes, rental costs and parking fees escalated in the surrounding areas, their dwellers began to covet neighboring property lying within the Lower North Side. Here the land was cheaper, rents were lower, and warehouse lofts could be converted into attractive offices or apartments. A real estate broker characterized the newcomers to the Lower North Side:

> Call them urban pioneers, greedy land-grabbers, or "yuppies" [young urban professionals] or whatever. They have been priced out of Lincoln Park, the lakefront Gold Coast and the upgraded downtown. They hunt for something new to create or rebuild. They revel in the chance and challenge to restore the old — on their modest budgets.

The new urban middle class is busily reclaiming inner city land which lies not only near the lakefront and its year-round attractions but also close to Chicago's business and governmental center downtown. The newcomers feel ill at ease with the vague, "Lower North Side" designation, a leftover from an unwanted past. Future-oriented and image-conscious, they seek to remove these inner city tracts from the shadow of Cabrini-Green and to bring them under some other neighborhood canopy. Every year by their presence they reduce the number of Lower North Side blocks still regarded as part of the social and physical environment of Cabrini-Green. Consequently, the foothills surrounding Cabrini-Green are more often earmarked River North, Old Town, Lincoln Park or LaSalle Drive West. These names identify the sections which have seceded from the Lower North Side and made another association.

These developments dissolved the identity of a community which would regard Cabrini-Green as its center. The new middle class on the Lower North Side enjoys being admonished that they are bucking the conventional urban wisdom, being admired for "living dangerously" and being watched over by friends not ready to take the same risks. The same real estate broker stressed that the Lower North Side newcomers

> are not like the owners of downtown office towers who built them like fortresses and ceded the pavements at night to the urban jungle. My Lower North Side newcomers are, of course, equally conscious of security in their smaller buildings. But there is a crucial difference. They are also streetwise. Aggressively, they seek to guarantee the safety of their streets in the evenings and on weekends. You know what? They are winning that battle over turf, wresting control of their sidewalks and streets from urban wolves.

13

Reclaiming the Slum

Each age is a dream that is dying. Or one that is coming to birth. —Arthur W.E. O'Shaughnessy, "Ode"

In the second half of the 20th century, the large, older cities of the United States launched an urban revolution whose proportions resemble those of the industrial upheaval of the 19th century. Cities today are not merely sprawling into suburbs; they are also rebuilding their historic urban cores. The inner city is once again being transformed, as it was during the rise of industrialism. The current reconstruction is as earthshaking as the earlier one.

Urban decay comes as no surprise. Cities age. They creak and tremble from thundering traffic on the ground and in the air, from the impact of newcomers or from advancing technology. When they develop middle-age spread, suburbs are born. The issue is not that cities decline; they inevitably do, like their aging citizenry. The perplexing question is: how are decrepit urban centers revitalized for the next century?

As Chicago approaches the year 2000, business leaders and government officials pour resources into the renewal of "old Chicago." That historic inner core, larger than Chicago's downtown, embraces as well adjoining areas to the south, west and north. Together these four sections make up not only Chicago's central area, but also the original ten square miles incorporated as the City of Chicago in 1837. (See map.)

Daniel Burnham, the architect after whom the Chicago Plan of 1909 was named, called this central area the "heart of Chicago."

152

Today that nucleus remains the vital center of a city now grown to 228 square miles, three million residents and fifty political wards. Commercially, the same central area is the nerve center of metropolitan Chicago covering 4,620 square miles in eight counties (including two in Indiana) and housing nearly eight million people.

The central section which was "old Chicago" has suffered from deterioration and from occasional panic ever since the 1950s. Would, for example, Chicago's downtown go the way of Newark, Detroit, St. Louis or Gary? In the 1980s it is undergoing rejuvenation. While the renovation is most visible along the lakefront, signs of renewal spring up everywhere in the central area. Still the heart of today's Chicago, this central area, covering less than five per cent of Chicago's turf, furnishes:

- forty per cent of all the jobs in Chicago;
- seventy per cent of all financial, insurance and real estate jobs in the entire Chicago region;
- employment in the private sector for almost a half-million workers, their number increasing each year; and
- jobs in the government sector for nearly 70,000 workers, nearly thirty per cent of Chicago's government employees.

To prosper as the hub of an eight-county metropolis, the central area of Chicago has had to develop new financial, cultural, commercial and governmental roles. These, in turn, require that the more compact business area known as Chicago's downtown expand its activity. In search of additional land and buildings, business leaders and government officials hurdle the Chicago River. There they find obsolete railroad properties and land devoted to warehousing and wholesaling. These underdeveloped acres, less than a mile from City Hall, also attract architects, real estate developers and urban pioneers, who energetically reclaim the land and buildings for new uses.

One of the central area's sub-sections, once readily recognized as the Lower North Side, is now the prime target of creeping renovation. This is the sub-section named as the "slum" in Zorbaugh's urban classic of 1929, *The Gold Coast and the Slum*. More than half a century later, what is now distinctive about this area is the threatening presence of a new slum, the Cabrini-Green public housing project. One of the city's largest high-rise projects, it lies closest to Chicago's downtown. Furthermore, it stands dramatically in the path of the onrushing revitalization which will inevitably compel City Hall to tackle the biggest single planning decision facing Chicago: the disposition of family high rises in Cabrini-Green and elsewhere.

The Latest Tug of War

Chicago history appears to side with the urban pessimist. In the many decades since 1837, the Lower North Side has survived, one way or another, as a third-rate residential area and, with some notable exceptions, as a second-class commercial section. The urban cynic's strongest arguments are drawn from the area's more recent history.

● Zorbaugh immortalized the Lower North Side as a "slum" in 1929, and ever since, the area has been stuck with that label.

● Giant private initiatives of the 1930s (the Merchandise Mart, the corporate headquarters of Montgomery Ward & Co. and the Marshall Field Garden Apartments) failed to redeem the area.

● The Marshall Field Garden Apartments, as they were originally called, were acclaimed in 1930 as a giant step in neighborhood rehabilitation under private sponsorship. For the last two decades, however, the 628-apartment complex, within walking distance of Cabrini-Green, survives as the largest parcel of privately owned blight in the area. Several attempts to upgrade living conditions and improve management have failed. In its present state, the housing complex, sometimes called "Cabrini-Green North," is a community eyesore, highly visible and an ever present threat to other housing rehabilitation and new construction nearby. In 1930 the complex drew a color line against black renters. Today, it no longer attracts white tenants; the residents are all black.

● Cabrini-Green, a massive rescue mission under government leadership in the 1940s and 1950s, did not succeed. As a result, the major caretaker of rental apartments on the Lower North Side is now a city agency, the Chicago Housing Authority. It has become the largest and most powerful slumlord in the history of Chicago. As a governmental agency, the CHA has been extremely reluctant to tamper with its huge supply of housing for the city's poorest households, and it has refused to do anything that might jeopardize the inflow of federal funds.

● The cascading deterioration of Cabrini-Green high rises has gone on since the 1960s, out of control and with no end in sight.

● During the last two decades city, state and federal agencies have spent in excess of $30 million on *special* programs to reduce juvenile delinquency, combat street crime, enhance resident security or improve education in Cabrini-Green. The assumption behind these programs was that the high-rise living could be improved enough to provide a decent living environment for children. Government bodies are no longer willing to risk large amounts of money for more new programs, when earlier ones had failed.

The Shrinking Slum

Urban optimists, however, come to a radically different conclusion. They argue that the social and economic conditions responsible for perpetuating Zorbaugh's slum are being removed one by one. They point out that his slum's privately owned blocks are now being replaced by new construction, rehabilitated loft buildings and refurbished offices, stores or galleries. Each year, therefore, the venerable slum grows smaller in size, its residents concentrated in the public housing project's 3,600 apartments. To justify their view of the Lower North Side as a shrinking slum, urban optimists rely on a variety of verifiable trends.

● Merchants, artists, church volunteers and others have accommodated themselves to Cabrini-Green, the myth and reality alike. Since their day-to-day experience produces few horror stories, they learn how to prosper in the immediate environment of the project. That is why Cabrini-Green's new neighbors continue to multiply each year. Nelson Forrest, executive director of the Greater North Michigan Avenue Association, echoes the prevailing sentiment:

> Cabrini-Green is not a major problem for us. It is, however, a major news concern. That publicity does present us with some problems.

● The Lower North Side no longer functions as a port of entry where cheap housing lures newly arrived immigrants. In Cabrini-Green and around it, the residents are increasingly second and third generation Chicagoans. Newcomers to Chicago now settle elsewhere in the city or its suburbs. Higher income families now settle in the area once known as the Lower North Side. They can afford to pay the rents in the new or renovated apartment buildings. They counterbalance the low-income character of the area so that it can now support shopkeepers, doctors and lawyers. Previously, the only viable business in the area was the currency exchange.

● The area's grimy industrial character, which once discouraged the construction of better dwellings, is being revamped, opening up new possibilities for private residential development. Many of the new apartments are rented to former residents of Cabrini-Green, who are able to demonstrate their upward mobility.

● The historic ethnic neighborhoods which were replaced, some forty years ago, by a low-income population of black residents are now becoming, except for Cabrini-Green, more cosmopolitan in occupancy, economically integrated, interracial and multi-ethnic.

● Clark Street's skid row, whose transient hotels, burlesque houses and saloons blighted not only that street but also LaSalle Drive and other adjoining blocks, has been dispersed. The streets in the new neighborhood are devoted to mixed uses, residential and commercial. Unlike many downtown streets, these are two-shift streets, used evenings and days by pedestrians, customers, visitors and residents alike.

● While the Lower North Side's inventory of substandard housing is steadily being depleted, its stock of standard housing grows — so that by the year 2000 the latter will exceed the former, reversing the current imbalance.

● Half a century of disinvestment in the Lower North Side is ending rapidly. New uses are being found for obsolete properties. And new buildings rise on vacant land. The urban bulldozer has become obsolete. Buildings are not razed wholesale for new development. Instead, new structures rise on already vacant lots or unused railroad land. Old factory buildings, empty for years, are converted to new uses. The displacement of people or businesses is a minor concern.

● With each decade sections of what once was unmistakably the territory of the Lower North Side instead become associated, unobtrusively, with the Lincoln Park community, the downtown business district or the westward extension of the lakefront Gold Coast. The Lower North Side will soon be left with very little land area that it can call its own.

● As industry and commerce are upgraded along the North Branch of the Chicago River, the riverside industries and businesses discover mutual interests and start elaborating an identity of their own. Slowly, they detach themselves from what is left of the Lower North Side.

● City-wide, many more Chicago voters better understand the hardships which beset children who live in a giant public housing project. These voters stand ready to condemn high-rise projects as incubators of the new social poverty. The ever-widening consensus is that most project families with children, whether they realize it or not, are better off living somewhere else.

● The block by block dismantling of the Lower North Side, via institutional bridge building or through annexation by neighboring communities goes forward. This dismembering has isolated Cabrini-Green homes, exposing it to intensive surveillance, locally and city-wide. As urban renovation and rebuilding approach on all sides, the housing project stands out like a medieval city under siege. Soon, Cabrini-Green will be all that remains of the Lower North Side slum. Furthermore, while the surrounding area undergoes spectacular improvement, conditions in the project itself worsen. The contrast becomes more unpromising each year.

A mother of four children who once had an apartment in Cabrini-Green and now lives two blocks from there, has no doubts about the signs of revitalization around her:

> You want to know what neighborhood improvement means? I'll tell you. Winning the dirty war against roaches and bedbugs. Starving the alley rats, poisoning them or forcing them to scavenge elsewhere. Abandoned and fire-bombed cars are towed away in a week. The street lights go on and off according to schedule. Curbs are repaired. Pot holes are fixed promptly. Sidewalks and even streets are swept clean by property owners. Lawns are kept up.

> Young hoodlums may toss their beer bottles and soft drink cans on the grassy parkways, but that litter doesn't stay there very long. Someone cares enough to pick up the litter and to box the ears of the litterer. Houses don't have broken windows or tottering fences. Apartment windows are clean and curtained. Door bells work. Mail boxes are unbroken. Back porches are sturdy and painted. Back yards look like gardens. If that is not neighborhood improvement, what is?

The block by block renewal closing in on Cabrini-Green in the 1980s is not as unplanned or as drastic as that resulting from the Chicago Fire of 1871. Nevertheless, revitalization today proceeds as surely as the rebuilding did a century ago. Only this time its purpose is to eradicate the last vestiges of a notorious slum. The current reclaiming of the Lower North Side furnishes a prototype for the renewing of other sections of "old Chicago," especially those dominated by large public housing projects obstructing further revitalization.

The Confrontation

The future of Cabrini-Green and the fate of the Lower North Side are entwined. As the Lower North Side fades away, the Cabrini-Green project, more visible and vulnerable, becomes the chief concern of reformers who live inside or outside the project. In the near future, therefore, the Cabrini-Green high rises will be at the center of a classic confrontation between political constituencies with clashing interests; between onrushing affluence and defensive poverty; between spunky owners of small properties and spineless bureaucracies; and between urban revival and inner city stagnation. Changes come slowly, allowing residents and businesses a chance to accommodate. The sudden, overnight destruction of properties by private or governmental action occurs infrequently.

Many who live or work in Cabrini-Green resist change. Thus far they have been unsuccessful in halting reclamation in the vicinity of Cabrini-Green. The status quo is defended by residents of Cabrini-Green who fear removal and by those whose jobs depend upon the persistence of poverty. Any wholesale eviction of Cabrini-Green tenants is seen as an intolerable option. But the gradual relocation of families with children, one high rise at a time, is not likely to arouse so powerful a protest that the status quo would remain undisturbed. Whether or not the CHA takes steps to upgrade the existing high rises, their life span remains precariously short. Were the CHA gradually to empty the Cabrini-Green high rises of children, so that they might enjoy the amenities of a walk-up apartment, the life of one or more of the high rises could be extended for other purposes.

At one time Cabrini-Green was viewed as the Near North Side's Rock of Gibraltar, but no longer. Hence, the Cabrini-Green public housing project faces an unsure future. Inevitably, Cabrini-Green's high rises will be recycled or torn down, their residents relocated. If the CHA ever manages to regain control of its Cabrini-Green apartments so that they are occupied only by bona fide tenants, the CHA will finally have an accurate count of its tenants. The CHA and City Hall can then begin long-range planning.

Those who want a front seat to view how "old Chicago" is being redeveloped should rivet their attention on the Near North Side. A visitor to Chicago in 1984 reacted to the changes he saw:

> I haven't been back to the Lower North Side for ten years. Then it looked like a disaster area, a Titanic in a sea of affluence.
>
> The new construction amazes me. The sparkling rehabilitation, both residential and commercial, chased away my earlier pessimism.
>
> Eyesores still abound. Dilapidation is there too. But the improvements stand out. Amazingly, I could ask, "Was a slum, dating back to the Great Chicago Fire, finally to expire?"

A city planner who had led the fight to preserve his own neighborhood situated elsewhere in the city, expressed astonishment at the corral of rejuvenated blocks ringing Cabrini-Green:

> These people are fearless. They won't be stopped. Some are black. Many are white. All earn good incomes. Are they the new urban pioneers? Like explorers, they edge their way closer and closer to the housing project.
>
> They buy or rent property; then they occupy it *personally.* That's what sets them apart from other speculators in urban real estate. They risk their own lives and property with the same iron determination that led 19th century farmers to settle the Illinois prairies.
>
> The early risk takers on the Lower North Side frontier are being followed by less adventurous settlers who, in another twenty years, will buy up every vacant lot and then build on it. The settlers will rent space in newly repaired buildings and put it to commercial and residential use. The mixed use ensures that the streets have traffic on them not just during the day but on evenings and weekends as well. They may even grow a neighborhood of their own.
>
> Nothing seems to detour them, even when they have to live or work down the street from Cabrini-Green. You know what? They are on a collision course with that housing project. When that day shows up, give me a front seat so that I can watch what happens.

The future of Chicago does not depend on the activity along its suburban edges. The urban frontier of the 1990s lies in the inner city — on the Near North Side and in other sections of "old Chicago" that encircle its downtown. Here 20th century pioneers struggle to reclaim the inner city as they rout the urban pessimist.

Postscript

For most of my adult life I have lived or worked on the Near North Side and have been involved with Cabrini-Green Homes. Early in 1982 with a Ford Foundation grant, I began writing this book. Someone had to make public the unfolding drama: the impending confrontation on the Near North Side over the future of the Cabrini-Green public housing project. *Reclaiming the Inner City* is an unfinished tale of the crunching changes underway.

My earliest brush with Cabrini-Green occurred in the 1940s. On behalf of the Catholic Interracial Council, Father Daniel M. Cantwell and I called on the pastor of St. Philip Benizi Church to seek an explanation for his refusal to admit a black child to the parish elementary school located next door to the new Cabrini row houses. This was twenty years before the civil rights revolution, when the Catholic chancery office seemed indifferent to racial discrimination in parish schools. The pastor's defense was candid. Builders of the Cabrini row houses were bulldozing the Italian parish he was striving to conserve and protect.

A few years later, the church building was torn down as the parish evaporated and the neighborhood disintegrated. The parish no longer exists, but the school building still stands and serves Cabrini-Green youngsters. It is now a tutoring and educational center operated by two church groups, CYCLE and the Fellowship of Friends, neither of which has a Catholic affiliation. They now own the school building, in exchange for a token payment to the Catholic Archdiocese of Chicago.

In the early 1950s, before the Cabrini high rises were erected, I edited a monthly newspaper called *Work*, published by the Catholic Labor Alliance. Through its pages we led an unsuccessful, city-wide campaign against the Chicago Housing Authority's foolish decision to go skyward with its public housing. At the time we were battling against high rises that were only nine stories high. In 1951 we editorialized:

> What scares us is that tall buildings always lead to more tall buildings. . . . Right now we are building slums for the future — this

time mammoth slums. However much they soar to heaven and look like temples to man-made gods, they are not eternal. . . .

What we want to know is: where is Chicago going to draw a line on further high-rise public housing? What we suggest is that Chicago draw it right now before we build any more cliff dwellings and skyscraper housing projects for families who want to raise children.

By 1958 Cabrini Homes had been extended with the addition of fifteen red-brick high rises, some nineteen stories high. They towered threateningly over the Cabrini row houses. In those days the most persuasive argument in favor of the high rises was that they were "better" than the slums they replaced. Today, does anyone doubt that living conditions in a high-rise project are excruciatingly worse than those in the slum which was demolished? Those who would preserve Cabrini-Green's high rises, at whatever the cost, operate from a dangerous and demoralizing assumption. They assume that a permanent underclass, from one generation to the next, is inevitable; and that our deteriorating high rises are needed to house — and hide — society's permanent poor. Those who would salvage the high rises for single-parent families with children on public assistance perpetuate the worst kind of poverty. Most Chicagoans, I contend, find such assumptions intolerable.

In the early 1960s, when I served as the director of the Chicago Commission on Human Relations, Monsignor John J. Egan and I took the new Archbishop of Chicago, Albert Gregory Meyer, to visit families in the row houses and high rises. It was a distressing experience for Archbishop Meyer. Cabrini's poverty was omnipresent and overwhelming. The stench of misery choked the air. What housing alternatives did low-income families have? Practically none, or so it seemed.

During the 1960s, I was a working partner in a consortium of public and private social agencies which had targeted the Cabrini-Green area for improvement. We generated a modest inflow of new private and federal dollars, the active involvement of residents and fresh initiatives from public officials, private agency staff and religious leaders concerned about the welfare of youth. But the program soon petered out. Cabrini-Green's problems had become monumental; our resources were minuscule; and the program approaches were not radical enough.

By 1970 another eight high rises had been added to the project. The new high rises, along with the earlier ones, quickly began to deteriorate. Social conditions were now far worse than in the 1960s. We put together a second consortium of public and private human service agencies, supported by funds from the federal government and private business. This time we sought to "individualize" five of the twenty-three high-rise buildings in Cabrini-Green. We hoped that residents would take greater responsibility for the conditions in the building in which they lived and would finally enjoy an address which they would be proud to acknowledge. After two years we could report moderate success — in lowering crime and vandalism, in increasing parental involvement and in opening new vistas for school-age children. In the third year our self-help program foundered. Federal and private funding shriveled. But more importantly, the Chicago Housing Authority was uncomfortable with the visible presence of private agency staff working directly with residents inside the high rises. Furthermore, the CHA was disturbed by a new assertiveness among tenants and was embarrassed that it did not control the multi-agency program in its own housing project. The CHA co-opted scarce federal dollars, took over the program, kept its trappings but neglected to involve the tenants individually. The program soon died. No one attended the funeral.

* * * * *

In completing the book I am in debt to many. To Howard Norris who recounts in Chapter VIII his journey through Cabrini-Green. Many of his insights have been incorporated into the book. To Betty Begg, Michelle Blees, Donna Ducharme, Kathy Hills, Kasia Marciniak, Virginia Marciniak, Christopher Maternowski, Diane Postilion and Mary Schiltz who will recognize the improvements they suggested but may still puzzle about conclusions I reach.

E.M.

Selected References

Devereux Bowly, Jr., *The Poorhouse: Subsidized Housing in Chicago, 1895-1976* (Carbondale, Ill.: Southern Illinois University Press, 1978).

Ernest W. Burgess and Charles Newcomb, Editors, *Census Data of the City of Chicago* (Chicago: University of Chicago Press, 1933).

Chicago Fact Book Consortium, Editors, *Local Community Fact Book: Chicago Metropolitan Area, Based on the 1970 and 1980 Censuses* (Chicago: Chicago Review Press, 1984).

Daphne Christensen, Editor, *Chicago Public Works: A History* (Chicago: Department of Public Works, 1973).

David Claerbut, *The Reluctant Defender: A Big-City Attorney Defends Desperate People* (Wheaton, Ill.: Tyndale House, 1978).

Irving Cutler, *Chicago: Metropolis of the Mid-Continent* (Dubuque: Kendall/Hunt, 1982, third edition).

Anthony Downs, *Opening Up the Suburbs* (New Haven: Yale University Press, 1973).

J.S. Fuerst, Editor, *Cabrini Extension Area: Portrait of a Slum* (Chicago: Chicago Housing Authority, 1951).

J.S. Fuerst, Editor, *Public Housing in Europe and America* (New York: John Wiley & Sons, 1974).

John Kenneth Galbraith, *The Affluent Society* (Boston: Houghton Miflin, 1969, revised second edition).

Michael Harrington, *The Other America* (New York: MacMillan, 1962).

James and Marti Hefley, *The Church That Takes on Trouble* (Elgin, Ill.: Cook Publishing, 1976).

Arnold R. Hirsch, *Making the Second Ghetto: Race and Housing in Chicago, 1940-1960* (New York: Cambridge University Press, 1983).

Allen H. Kelson, Editor, *Chicago Magazine's Guide to Chicago* (Chicago: Contemporary Books, Inc., 1983).

Evelyn M. Kitagawa and Karl E. Taeuber, Editors, *Local Community Fact Book: Chicago Metropolitan Area, 1960* (Chicago: Chicago Community Inventory, University of Chicago, 1963).

Charles P. Livermore, Editor, *Historic City: The Settlement of Chicago* (Chicago: Department of Planning, 1976).

Ed Marciniak, *Reversing Urban Decline: The Winthrop-Kenmore Corridor in the Edgewater and Uptown Communities of Chicago* (Washington, D.C.: National Center for Urban Ethnic Affairs, 1981).

Ed Marciniak, *Reviving an Inner City Community: The Drama of Urban Change in East Humboldt Park in Chicago* (Washington, D.C.: National Center for Urban Ethnic Affairs, 1977).

Harold M. Mayer and Richard C. Wade, *Chicago: Growth of a Metropolis* (Chicago: University of Chicago Press, 1969).

Martin Meyerson and Edward Banfield, *Politics, Planning and the Public Interest: The Case of Public Housing in Chicago* (Glencoe: Free Press, 1955).

Herman P. Miller, Editor, *Poverty American Style* (Belmont, Cal.: Wadsworth, 1966).

Municipal Reference Library Staff, *Historical Information about Chicago* (Chicago: Municipal Reference Library, 1975).

Thomas Lee Philpott, *The Slum and the Ghetto: Neighborhood Deterioration and Middle-Class Reform, Chicago, 1880-1930* (New York: Oxford University Press, 1978)

Alex Polikoff, *Housing the Poor* (Cambridge: Ballinger Publishing Co., 1978).

Jacob A. Riis, *How the Other Half Lives* (New York: Charles Scribner & Sons, 1914).

Raymond J. Struyk, *A New System for Public Housing: Salvaging A National Resource* (Washington: Urban Institute, 1980).

Mitchell Sviridoff, *Human Resources and the Pendulum of Power* (New York: Ford Foundation, 1976).

Richard P. Taub, D. Garth Taylor, Jan D. Dunham, *Paths of Neighborhood Change: Race and Crime in Urban America* (Chicago: University of Chicago Press, 1984).

U.S. House of Representatives, Committee on Ways and Means, subcommittee on public assistance and unemployment compensation, *Background Material on Poverty,* October 17, 1983.

Elizabeth Wood, *The Beautiful Beginnings, The Failure to Learn: Fifty Years of Public Housing in America* (Washington, D.C.: National Center for Housing Management, 1982).

Harvey Warren Zorbaugh, *The Gold Coast and the Slum* (Chicago: University of Chicago Press, 1929).

Index